Caring for

Infants and Toddlers in Groups:

*Developmentally
Appropriate Practice*

J. Ronald Lally, Abbey Griffin,
Emily Fenichel, Marilyn Segal,
Eleanor Szanton, and Bernice Weissbourd

ZERO TO THREE

Contents

Acknowledgments *4*

Introduction *5*

SECTION I.
Development in the First Three Years of Life *7*

SECTION II.
Components of Quality Infant/toddler Child Care *29*

SECTION III.
Infant/toddler Group Care in Context *45*

Summary *57*

Illustrations of Appropriate and Inappropriate
Practice *59*

Developmental Milestones of the First Three Years *78*

References and Resources *80*

Acknowledgments

THE AUTHORS GRATEFULLY ACKNOWLEDGE Janice Molnar and the Ford Foundation for the encouragement and support that have made this publication possible. We are especially grateful to the staff of the Program for Infant/Toddler Caregivers, both those at Far West Laboratory (Peter Mangione, Sheila Signer, and Terry DeMartini) and those at the California Department of Education (Janet Poole and Mary Smithberger). They developed many of the concepts and documents upon which Section II is based. We thank Nancy P. Alexander and Janet Brown McCracken for their skillful matching of photographs to concepts; Amy Dombro and Donna Wittmer for telling us about "Richie and his cello" and "Haniya at the sink;" the California Parent Services Program and the Boston City Hospital Child Witness to Violence Project for illustrating infant/toddler group care in context; and the Advisory Committee on Services to Families with Infants and Toddlers for conceptualizing child development, family development, staff development, and community building as the four essential cornerstones of any service designed to support infants, toddlers, and their families.

The authors are deeply grateful to the reviewers who offered us a wealth of insights and wisdom: Kay Albrecht, Nancy P. Alexander, Nancy Balaban, Sonya Bemporad, Elsbeth Brown, Maria Chavez, Laura J. Colker, Jerlean Daniels, Louise Derman-Sparks, Diane Dodge, Amy Dombro, Mary Dudley, Jane Grady, Thelma Harms, Shelley Heekin, Nell Ishee, Lisa Jakob, Kadija Johnston, Carol Klass, Elizabeth Memel, Susan Ord, Carol Brunson Phillips, Eva Thorp, Louis Torrelli, Yolanda Ledon Torres, and Donna Wittmer.

Sue Bredekamp's enduring commitment to excellence in the early care and education of all young children provides us with a steady beacon to follow. We also gratefully acknowledge the trailblazing work of the late Nancy Travis. The memory of Sally Provence, former president of ZERO TO THREE and co-author of the original version of this publication, informs and inspires everything we do.

Introduction

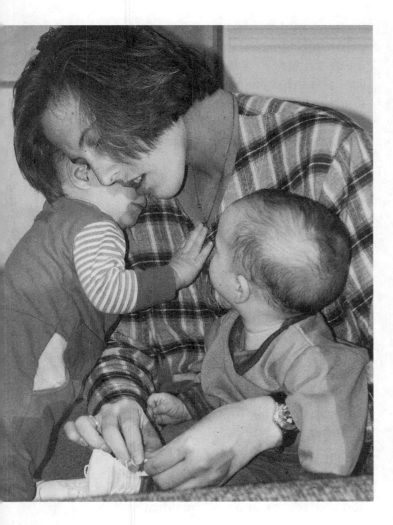

HIGH-QUALITY GROUP CARE for infants and toddlers can enrich children's early experience and provide critical support to their families. Yet caring for children from birth to three in groups presents special challenges—challenges that are related to the very characteristics which make the first three years of life a unique period in human development:

• In these years, development and emerging identity unfold day by day in the context of the baby's relationships with a few caring adults.

• In these years, children are vulnerable; they have not developed the capacity to cope actively with internal or external stress and discomfort.

• In these years, physical, social, emotional, and cognitive development are more intertwined than later in life.

• In these years, growth in all domains of development is far more rapid than during any other period of life. The baby or toddler's needs and interests at any moment are the best guide to what will support emerging abilities.

Developmentally appropriate programs for children from birth to age 3 require special knowledge, skill, and program design. Just as a good preschool is not a scaled-down version of elementary classrooms, so too, a good infant/toddler program is distinctly different from a program designed for 3 -5 year-olds. Group care for infants and toddlers is demanding work. It requires both careful planning, informed by knowledge of development in the earliest years, and the flexibility to respond to the individual needs of each child and family.

The key to quality care is the quality of relationships—relationships between the infant and her family, between child and caregiver, between caregiver and family, and among adults in the child care setting. Child care quality depends on caregivers who are knowledgeable and skilled, and committed to creating and sustaining these relationships.

Unfortunately, current practices in many infant/toddler child care settings hinder caregivers, children, and families from forming and sustaining the deep, responsive, and respectful relationships that are the hallmark of quality. *Caring for Infants and Toddlers in Groups: Developmentally Appropriate Practice* is designed to help caregivers, program directors, coordinators, administrators, trainers, licensors, families, and leaders in the field of early care and education recognize—and communicate to others—the knowledge and skills that are needed to offer a nurturing group care environment that supports the healthy development of very young children. By illustrating the experiences and dilemmas that young children, caregivers, and families face every day, we hope to suggest the tremendous opportunities for development that good group care offers to children and adults alike.

Gender pronouns (he and she), are used interchangeably to stress the individuality of each child as well as to remind us that both women and men provide infant and toddler child care.

Section I of this guide provides an overview of children's development in the first three years. It offers illustrations of how infant/toddler caregivers respond to the rapid pace and many individual variations of development, and of how caregivers and families can work together to support infants' and toddlers' healthy growth in the context of group care.

Section II examines eight components of quality in group care for infants and toddlers, with illustrations from the daily experience of children, caregivers, and families in centers and family child care.

Section III places infant/toddler child care in the context of a community network of supports and services for families with young children. It describes child development, family development, staff development, and community building as "stars" in a constellation of comprehensive, individualized supports and services in the community.

Illustrations of appropriate and inappropriate practice offer examples of interactions among adults and children, family/caregiver interactions, arrangement of the physical environment, selection and use of equipment, health and safety policies and procedures, and staff qualifications.

SECTION 1

Development in the First Three Years of Life

DURING THE PAST 30 YEARS, careful observation of infants and toddlers around the world has yielded an ever-increasing awareness of the importance of early development. Every day, it seems, we learn more about the capacities of newborns, the differences among very young children, the influence of family and community culture on early development, and the ability of infants and toddlers to cope with developmental challenges. We are also learning that group care of infants and toddlers presents special challenges and opportunities for promoting healthy development and supporting families.

Perhaps most important, we have learned to appreciate the role of relationships in every aspect of early development. Infants and toddlers develop expectations about people's behavior and about themselves based on how parents and others treat them. Through daily interactions with responsive, affectionate adults, babies experience their first positive love relationships. Trust and emotional security develop when infants learn that their needs will be met predictably and consistently. Self-confidence develops as babies and toddlers learn to communicate their needs and master challenges in their world.

Infants and toddlers thrive when they encounter challenges they can meet. Infants flourish when they are free to explore, and when they feel that caring adults encourage and take pleasure in their emerging interests and skills. Children's sense of belonging and ability to understand their world grow when there is continuity between the home and child care setting.

The overview of infant and toddler development that follows offers a series of snapshots of babies' growing capacities, the experiences of children and parents, and what the family-caregiver relationship might look like at different points in the first three years. Readers are encouraged to consult the references and resources section of this document, which includes classic studies of early development, recent works, and ongoing sources for new information.

Although there are many ways to define and describe "ages and stages" within the rapid course of development in the first three years, we have chosen to look at three periods, characterized by mobility and age range:

- **young infants** (birth to 9 months);
- **mobile infants** (8 to 18 months); and
- **toddlers** (16 to 36 months).

Each section describes what can generally be expected of the child, the appropriate response of the caregiver, and how families and caregivers work together (the "alliance"). Thus, each age range has three subsections: the child, the caregiver, and the alliance.

The overlap in ages reminds us of the importance of individual differences among young children's rates of development. Chronological age alone is not a good indicator of child development but is used here to remind us that the competent caregiver will need to provide different environments, experiences, and interactions for children as they grow.

Regardless of their level of development, infants need a caregiver's help in each stage, as they learn about security, exploration, and identity. During the different stages of infancy and early childhood, the type of help children need will change. For example, caregiver practices that help young infants feel secure (keeping a child physically close) can thwart a mobile infant's emerging urge to explore or block a toddler from learning more about how to depend on herself. Developmentally appropriate practice with infants and toddlers requires the ability to adapt a pattern of care quickly to meet children's rapidly changing needs.

● ● ● ● ●
Young Infants *(birth to nine months)*
● ● ● ● ●

The baby from birth to 8 or 9 months of age needs
security most of all. The young infant thrives on
the warmth and caring that come from a close relationship with the caregiver. Feelings about security
influence the baby's inclination to explore and become part of the child's identity. Young infants
need to know that someone special will come
promptly when they feel distressed. Learning that
they can count on being cared for helps babies
build a sense of security.

● The child

Every baby is unique. Newborns differ in their biological rhythms and the way they use their senses
(sight, hearing, touch, smell, and taste) to learn
about the world around them. They differ in their
responses to loud noises or sudden changes in
lighting and in the ways they like to be held. What
all newborns share is a need for good health,
safety, warm, loving relationships with their primary caregivers, and care that is responsive to
their individual differences.

Babies enter the world ready for relationships.
They use sounds, facial expressions, and movements to communicate their needs and feelings.
Very young infants show a particular interest in the
people around them. They like to look and listen;
they follow the father's voice as well as the
mother's. They look intently at the light and dark
contours of the human face, and can discriminate
between an accurate drawing of a human face and
one in which the main features are out of place.

Babies a few months old show their pleasure and involvement with a caregiver through looking, joyful smiling and laughing, arm and leg movements, and other gestures.

Babies delight in hearing language. They coo when talked to and develop different types of cries to express different needs. Long before they speak in words, infants coo, then babble, then make sounds that imitate the tones and rhythms of adult talk, particularly those of their families and home culture. Before they understand even simple word combinations, they read gestures, facial expressions and tone of voice. Babies begin quickly to participate in the turn-taking of conversation. For example, as young infants, they vocalize as a partner in a conversation—one partner talks, one listens; if one disengages, the other calls her back into the dialogue. Some particularly social babies can be observed "conversing" with each other.

Babies learn through movement. As they move their arms, legs, and other body parts, and through touching and being touched, babies become more aware of how their bodies move and feel. They soon discover they can change what they see, hear, or feel through their own activity—how delightful to kick, and then see the mobile move!

Young infants become deeply engrossed in the practice of a newly discovered skill, like putting their hands together to grasp an object. Through the repetition of actions, they develop their motor skills and physical strength. They explore objects, people, and things by kicking, reaching, grasping, pulling, and releasing objects by opening their hands.

Babies use their senses and emerging physical skills to learn about the people and objects around them; they engage their senses by touching different textures and putting things in their mouths. They learn to anticipate how familiar adults will respond to them, a skill that will evolve much later

Ben and Jennifer started at the child care center at 4 months of age and were assigned the same primary caregiver. Ben was quiet and calm, unaffected by sudden occurrences and gracious about waiting to be fed. Jennifer was his opposite. Jen was tight-bodied and highly sensitive to changes in her environment. She cried loudly and persistently when hungry, sleepy or upset. Their caregiver, Teresa, and respective family members saw that after only a month together, at 5 months of age, Ben and Jen were fascinated by each other. One would light up when the other arrived—Ben smiling and opening his eyes wide with anticipation; Jennifer wiggling every part of her body, making high-pitched sounds. Lying on their tummies looking at each other was a favorite activity. Both would arch their backs and heads until they could hold them up no more, then collapse. When one was face down, the other would use body and voice to summon the partner back.

Ben and Jennifer's primary caregiver and parents were keen observers and ready to follow the interests of their babies. Teresa encouraged the interaction by putting them face to face when both were alert and active. Besides the very early show of mutual interest, Teresa noticed that they had a positive effect on each other. Often Jen could be soothed by Ben's calm presence; in return, Ben was enlivened by Jen's passion.

into an ability to "read" people and anticipate how to behave in new situations. Ideally, young infants are learning that their needs are understood and will be met. They are learning that new skills and new experiences most often bring pleasure and that with determined efforts they will succeed—and, most important, that those they love will share in the joys of their discoveries. These early experiences affect a child's approach to learning far into the future.

The caregiver

It is through responsive interactions with parents and a few other special caregivers that infants develop a sense of a safe, interesting and orderly world where they are understood and their actions bring pleasure to themselves and others. Like dancers, the caregiver and infant synchronize their interactions, each responding to and influencing the other.

Because each baby is unique, the caregiver's task is to learn the baby's individual eating and sleeping rhythms, how she approaches new objects and people, and how she prefers to be held for feeding, sleeping or comforting. While the adult becomes able to predict what the infant needs and how he will respond to different kinds of stimuli, the baby is learning what to expect. The infant's sense of safety, security, and confidence grows with her sense that the people and the world about her are predictable and offer interesting experiences.

The young infant's day revolves around caregiving routines—diapering, dressing, eating, and sleeping. Caregiving routines are important times, offering unique opportunities for one-to-one interaction, and for visual and tactile learning. In the child care setting, each area where these routines take place must be carefully planned so that the caregiver's time in preparation and sanitation procedures, like getting needed supplies and careful handwashing, can be handled efficiently, leaving more time for interaction with the baby. Pictures and objects at the infant's eye level capture his interest, while clean, safe, warm surfaces help him feel comfortable and secure. When routines are pleasurable, infants learn that their needs and their bodies are important.

Young infants need many opportunities to sample a variety of sensory and motor experiences. Before they can creep or crawl, babies depend on adults to carry them to, or present them with an interesting object or activity. However, too much stimulation (bright lights, too many children in one group, constant loud noise, too many objects in a clutter) can be overwhelming. A well-organized environment, where objects are placed on low shelves, and where there is a variety of visual, tactile and physically challenging choices to capture the infant's attention, encourages curiosity, exploration, and lets each infant engage his world at his own pace.

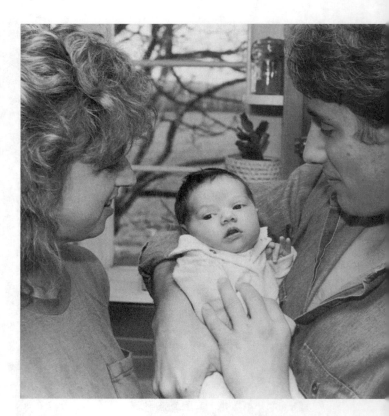

The caregiver/family alliance

Entering child care is a transition that, among other things, means building new relationships. By the time an infant enters group care, parents have learned a great deal about their baby. The baby has also learned. She has learned to expect a certain pattern of response from her immediate family—a pattern that reflects the values, culture, and child-rearing beliefs of the family and community. The infant will expect this pattern from her primary caregiver in the group care setting. It will take time for her to adjust to differences in touch, tone of voice, and the sights and sounds of a new environment.

To build solid relationships at the beginning of an infant's child care experience, caregivers need to learn from the experiences, knowledge, culture, and child-rearing beliefs of family members. When caregivers value the family as the primary caregivers and the constant in the baby's life, the parent-caregiver relationship becomes one of mutual support and learning about how best to care for the infant or toddler. An alliance is created.

Establishing and maintaining the alliance between parent and caregiver require regular communication. The caregiver sets aside time, particularly at the beginning and/or end of the baby's day, to communicate with parents through written notes, telephone calls, casual conversation, and scheduled meetings. Thus, family and caregiver can keep abreast of the baby's health; sleeping, eating, and elimination patterns; interests; and accomplishments. The knowledgeable caregiver can anticipate new developmental challenges and help the parent adjust to the changes in behavior and moods that often accompany a baby's intense effort to master a new skill.

Families and caregivers of young infants may have different perspectives on what a baby needs or on the best way to meet his needs. The skilled caregiver watches for such differences and approaches them as opportunities to learn more about the family and their community. These are opportunities to build the alliance, creating for the baby an environment that reflects his home experience.

The caregiver uses her observational skills to learn more about the individual baby's needs, interests, preferences, and particular ways of responding to people and things. Communication skills help the caregiver learn from the baby's family how his behaviors and reactions reflect his individual style, physical needs, and his home experience. Communication skills, which take time and

David's (7 months) family's pediatrician had suggested a strict daily eating and sleeping schedule because the baby was very active and easily distracted. Mattie, the family child care provider, adopted the routine, but as she got to know David, she became increasingly convinced that he needed a more flexible schedule. At first, she simply reported to David's parents that she had a hard time getting David to sleep, or that he was very cranky and hungry a half-hour before his scheduled feeding time, or that he got very angry when she insisted he finish his bottle. But soon, because she felt she was failing David and was ignoring the two toddlers she also cared for, she decided to have a serious discussion with his parents about the possibilities of giving up the fixed schedule. Sitting in her living room, Mattie described what she observed and asked whether either parent was seeing similar behavior at home. They said that, while they thought the schedule was worth trying, they too were beginning to recognize early signs of hunger or fatigue and that David seemed much happier when they responded right away. Mattie was relieved, and began to talk freely about ways to catch David's early signs and reduce possible distractions so that he could learn to follow his own body signals.

Mattie was relieved, because such negotiations do not always go so well. There are many reasons parents might want a particular routine—it is what they know from their own upbringing; it may be valued in their culture; they may have read something that suggested this approach was best for their baby; or, as in David's case, a health professional may have suggested the schedule. David's parents came from a community in which medical professionals were highly respected authorities. This caregiver's good communication skills, conviction based on careful observation, knowledge of child development, and respectful approach helped her and David's families trust their own shared, developing understanding of this particular child's emerging needs. "Talking through the child," as Mattie did, is a communication technique that uses observed behaviors to keep parents focused on their child. It is a way to avoid slipping into a confrontation about who knows what is best for the child—a kind of competition the experienced caregiver knows is almost never productive.

training to develop, also help the caregiver discuss differences openly with the family and arrive at a mutually satisfying agreement. This becomes easier as the family-caregiver relationship grows stronger.

Leaving your young infant in the care of someone else is difficult. Parents feel differently about this experience and express their feelings in different ways. Some are clearly grieving and need emotional support and reassurance. Others steel themselves by acting aloof; they may even appear uncaring. Still others become overbearing "managers," sometimes competitive with the caregiver, often demanding. To become sensitive to differences in how parents express their feelings requires time and training.

Infants and toddlers evoke strong feelings in adults—both family members and caregivers. Recognizing, accepting and working to overcome conflicting feelings is one of the major challenges of sharing care. Communicating with all parents regularly and taking every opportunity to reflect their baby's need and love for them will help parents leave their baby in the child care setting comfortably while staying emotionally close, certain that they are still the most important people in their baby's lives.

Young infants thrive on responsive caregiving, a stimulating environment and unhurried time to experience the simple joys of relating. Knowledge of early development and skill in observation help both parents and caregivers be more responsive to babies, whose needs and moods and interests vary from moment to moment. The alliance between parent and caregiver has many benefits for the adults, but, most important, it helps them provide better and more responsive care for the baby.

Samantha (3 months) had been a fussy baby and her parents and caregiver had learned to respond quickly to the first signals of hunger, fatigue or wet diaper discomfort because her cries became unbearably loud within seconds. One day her mother entered the center grinning. She reported with pride that she awoke to Samantha's first morning call for breast feeding; she had rushed to the crib, saying, "Mommy's coming, I know you're hungry. Mommy's coming." Rather than the usual red-faced screaming baby, she found Samantha with her thumb in her mouth, intently watching her kicking feet. Samantha had learned to soothe and entertain herself. In their excitement, caregiver and parent marveled at Samantha's new mastery and shared words and responses they might use to build on her trust. They talked about ways Samantha could build her repertoire of self-soothing behaviors.

This parent and caregiver clearly have a good relationship. One of the many rewards of such a relationship are the opportunities for shared enthusiasm. Another is that through sharing their observations and thoughts, parents and caregivers can learn from each other. When one discovers a caregiving strategy that works, the other can follow suit. This creates continuity and reinforces the baby's ability to anticipate adult responses to her needs.

Very young infants are frequently fussy as their central nervous system, digestive system and other physical capacities develop. Depending on how adults respond, infants learn very different lessons about themselves and their world. Responsive, consistent care helped Samantha trust that those who loved her would relieve her distress. When physically capable and emotionally and cognitively ready, she could soothe her own physical discomfort, trusting that the sound of a familiar voice meant that relief was on its way.

Samantha's first successful attempt at self-soothing reflects multiple domains of learning. Physically, Samantha is using her thumb to satisfy the urge to suck and her kicking to distract her from her hunger. Cognitively, she can now associate the adult's voice with relief. Socially, she has taken an important step towards self-regulation and will receive the rewards of happier and more relaxed caregiving. Emotionally, she has taken a giant step toward trust and attachment, gaining a new sense of both her own competence and the trustworthiness of others. When the caregiver understands such normal developmental challenges and achievements in the first nine months of life, she can offer encouragement, insight, and support to both infants and family members.

Mobile Infants *(eight to 18 months)*

Exploration takes center stage as the infant becomes more mobile. Often curious and on the move, the mobile infant seems to get into everything in a quest to learn more about the world.

The mobile infant begins to build an identity as an explorer and increasingly ventures out when she feels secure. Caregivers can provide trustworthy support and encouragement to mobile infants by making eye contact with them, talking with them, and gesturing to them. Under a warm and watchful eye, mobile infants will develop feelings of confidence and competence. It is important for caregivers to remember that at this stage infants **practice** independence but very much need trusted adults as a secure base of support.

● The child

Mobility opens new worlds for infants. They can now move to what or whom they want by scooting, using their hands and bouncing forward; commando-crawling with stomach on the ground; one-legged stand-crawling; crawling on all fours; walking with assistance, and, finally, toddling. For the mobile infant, the world is full of inviting experiences. Most are exciting, challenging or pleasurable. Some are painful, frustrating or frightening. Freedom to move about safely is vital for infants who are beginning to crawl or walk.

Mobile infants are fascinated with the daily activities and belongings of the adults around them. They imitate, holding a comb to a doll's head, patting an adult's cheek to comfort as they have experienced comfort, and mimicking facial expressions of sadness or anger they have seen. Imitation is the first step into the world of dramatic play, in which the child practices what she experiences and sees. During this period of development, infants create mental images of how things work and of sequences of adult behaviors that will soon become part of their rich repertoire of dramatic play themes.

Infants at this stage make use of new physical, cognitive, social, and emotional abilities, and the connections among them, to discriminate between familiar and unfamiliar people, and to seek an object or person that is out of sight. Playing peek-a-boo or hide and seek and finding an object hidden in a box are among the many ways infants explore this new understanding of how the world of objects and people works. While they respond with differing degrees of intensity, based on both individual temperament and experiences, almost all infants during this period show anxiety ("stranger fear") around unfamiliar people. A clown face, Santa Claus, a firefighter in uniform, or a mask can be terrifying. Infants at this age can be fearful and upset when a trusted adult leaves their sight.

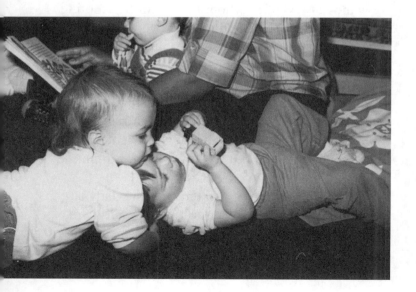

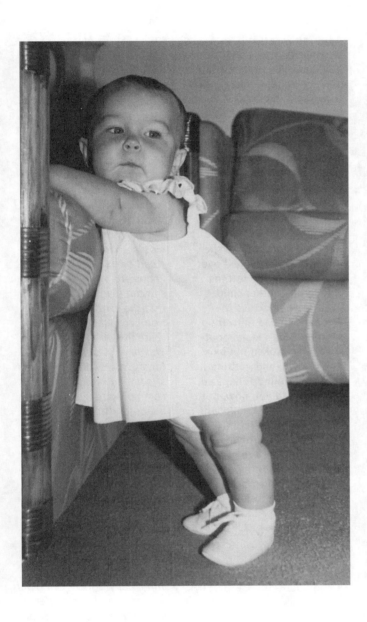

While distressing to infants and the adults who love them, these powerful emotions reflect new social, emotional, and cognitive understanding. Mobile infants recognize that they are separate people from their caregivers. They express their strong emotional ties to the adults they love, and they are acutely aware of their vulnerability when their loved ones are gone. A cherished object (a "lovey"), like a blanket, a piece of their parent's clothing, or a stuffed toy can be very helpful as mobile infants navigate this very complicated and important emotional voyage towards independence.

As they play, mobile infants can be totally absorbed. Opening and shutting, filling and dumping, and picking up and dropping are all activities that challenge infants' mobility and dexterity as well as their ideas about objects and what they can do. Physical activity and learning are intricately connected, as infants discover, test, and confirm that objects can be out of sight (inside a box or in a cabinet) and then found; that objects can be all together, separated into pieces, and put together again; and that adults can be resources for reaching what has been dropped.

During this period, infants develop small muscle skills as they grasp, drop, pull, push, throw, and mouth objects. They develop their large muscles as they creep, crawl, cruise, walk holding onto furniture, climb up onto couches and ramps, and descend stairs. Learning to sit unassisted marks infants' readiness to do things for themselves (as they see adults and older children doing), like feeding themselves and playing with blocks, water, or other materials.

Through their exploration of objects and their own physical skills, mobile infants learn rudimentary rules of cause and effect, the use of objects as tools for specific purposes, sequence, classification, and spatial relationships. They begin to group and compare. They use and manipulate tools—for example, using a cup to scoop water.

The mobile infant is both practicing independence and testing new ways to stay connected to those she loves and trusts to protect her as she moves about on her own. Eye contact, vocalizing, and gesturing take on added importance as tools for maintaining that connection. A strong, loving relationship with a trusted adult gives the mobile infant the secure base from which he can explore his world.

The caregiver

Mobile infants' new abilities and understandings have a profound effect on relationships between them and their primary caregivers. Infants can now move away from, and back to, the security of a loving adult. They can get to an attractive object or place on their own, but as they play, they maintain their sense of security by checking in with their primary caregiver through eye contact, a coo, or a gesture. They rely on loving, vigilant adults to create an environment safe for exploration and to reassure them of their safety.

By the time they become mobile, babies have already learned a great deal about language and communication. Now they begin to understand the meaning of words. With language a new era of relatedness emerges. Their earliest words reflect their social environment—usually the names of important adults, objects, and activities associated in their daily lives. In response, caregivers slow down their own speech and enunciate words clearly. Expanding, repeating, labeling, and using words from the infant's primary language are among the many ways adults help infants add new words to their repertoire and encourage their sense of themselves as effective communicators.

Joan (10 months) was in motion. She used a large yellow truck to pull herself up to a standing position, dropped to her knees, crawled and scooted about the room, crawled up the two-step platform, sat for a moment to survey the room, and called to Gina, her primary caregiver, with her eyes. They smiled at each other. Joan rolled onto her tummy and slid down the carpeted steps, where she sat and, again, looked over toward Gina. When Gina picked up another child, Joan crawled across the floor,and pulled herself up holding Gina's knee, pouting. Gina stroked her hair, knelt down, and, putting her free arm around Joan, said, "I can't hold you now, but I can come watch while you climb up." Joan returned Gina's smile, burrowed her head into Gina's thigh, then crawled back to the platform. She looked back to be sure Gina had followed and called, "Ji! Ji! Ji!" in an excited voice.

This baby and her caregiver have many ways of communicating. Eye contact is mutual and regular. Adult and child are in tune and check in regularly. A gesture of the arms, a sound, or a pout expresses to the adult what Joan needs. Gina responds gesturally (by putting her arm around Joan to soothe her and reinforce their connection) and also puts Joan's physical communication into words. Joan does not understand the words, but she knows from the tone and all she can read in Gina's face that she can have her attention even when she has to share it with another baby. This brief interaction reinforces Joan's sense of herself as someone who is able to communicate, get what she needs, and control intense feelings—and whose achievements are valued by an adult she loves and trusts.

The younger baby in Gina's arms benefits from the interaction as well. From his perch, he can watch and share in the excitement about skills he has not yet developed. "Ordinary" interactions between an adult and a baby or between older and younger infants offer important opportunities for learning. For example, Joan's desire to use words to communicate grows as she hears Gina talk; the younger baby can share the excitement of physical feats he can not yet perform.

The mobile infant whose family speaks a different language than the caregiver will feel supported in using her home language if caregivers learn some key words and songs from her family and get simple picture books with captions in the family's language.

Listening is a critical skill for effective communication that adults can model even as the infant expresses herself in "babble talk," with a few identifiable words. The caregiver demonstrates her interest in understanding the infant by listening, watching, and giving words to the child. The question, "You want the truck?" reinforces the infant's sense that she can communicate her needs and wishes to others. The joy in her eyes when her words are understood, or when she hears the caregiver use words spoken at home tells of her excitement and eagerness to join and become competent in this important aspect of the adult world.

Mobile infants are naturally very curious about other children. Friendships are beginning to emerge. Because infants are not yet experienced in interacting with each other, they often require assistance. A mobile infant will grab at another's hair and pull at his clothes with the same interest she shows in sharing a picture book or crawling up a ramp side by side.

Because mobile infants can be so easily stimulated, sensitive adults will ensure that a good balance is maintained in the levels of intensity of play, from active . . . to quiet . . . to sleep. The developmentally appropriate environment supports the infant's new mobility, interest in routines, imitation of the behaviors of adults and older children, and capacity to engage in a wider range of activities. Structures (e.g., low platforms, tunnels) invite the infant to pull herself up, take steps, climb up steps or risers, and crawl into partially enclosed spaces to gain new perspectives on the world. Spaces are organized to invite specific types of activities (a

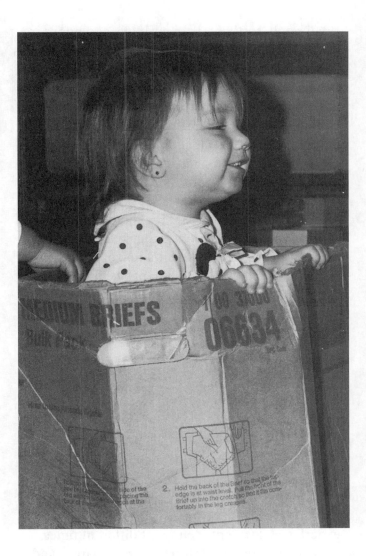

small nook, softly lit, with cushions and books in pockets hung on the wall, says to the baby, "This is a place for quiet activities, books are special, and I am protected while I 'read'.")

Ensuring health and safety, always a major concern in group care, demands extra precautionary measures when mobile infants are involved. Caregivers must check the environment regularly for potential dangers. Splinters, unlocked cabinets containing cleaning materials, uncovered electrical outlets, pot handles within the infant's reach, small objects, pieces of balloons, a purse left open, and medications left out, are but a few of the long list of potential threats to the infant's health or safety.

The caregiver/family alliance

The mobile infant, his family members, and his caregiver are entering a stage of development that is laced with complicated feelings about separation and attachment, much excitement, and many challenges. At one moment, the baby is consumed with his own movement, crawling, scooting, or toddling off with abandon. In the next, he is fighting to keep the adult close, crying if left for a moment. Each partner in the triangle of relationships may experience different feelings at different times; thus honest communication between parent and caregiver takes on added importance. Working together, they can keep their focus on what is most important for the infant. They can identify and experiment with ways to maintain his sense of security in the child care setting, reinforcing daily his understanding that his parents will be back, that they still love him, and that his caregiver will love and protect him while his family is away.

As with young infants, open and frequent communication is needed to assure continuity between family and caregiver. Parents and caregivers of mobile infants must keep pace with their rapid development by changing the environment and making decisions about how to encourage mobility, independence, and curiosity within safe boundaries. Negotiations with families must be guided by the caregiver's commitment to reaching a mutual understanding. A mutual understanding of the use of "no" is a good example. While mobile infants might be encouraged by the caregiver to use "no" as a tool for self-defense and a statement of independence, many families do not believe that it is appropriate to allow a young child to say "no." In some cultures, such statements of independence, especially when directed toward an adult, are viewed as highly inappropriate. Cultural beliefs and rules about infants' self-feeding, being "loud," and moving without restraint also vary.

The caregiver who anticipates that cultural and child rearing beliefs will differ among families is ready to open communication. If their beliefs conflict, a caregiver and family can find a mutually acceptable approach by talking over a range of strategies until they reach consensus. This requires strong communication skills on the part of the caregiver as well as a belief that family members are the primary caregivers and a constant, powerful influence on the child's development. The skilled caregiver realizes that being a competent professional requires the ability to listen carefully, explore the parent's perspective fully, and steer the conversation to areas of agreement.

Some parents and caregivers experience deep feelings of loss as the infant becomes more independent. Others feel relief. Whatever feelings are aroused by a young child's development, the alliance between caregiver and parent can be tremendously helpful, as each gives support and insights to the other.

As a young infant, Maya had moved easily through morning and evening transitions in her family child care, and a warm relationship had developed between Marina, Maya's mother, and Shanita, the family child care provider. At 16 months, however, Maya began clinging to Shanita in the evening, unwilling to let her mother hold her. If Marina arrived while Maya was playing, she was greeted with tears. One evening, when Marina was trying to pick Maya up to go, Shanita, feeling Marina's hurt and concern, stepped in, saying: "You know, Marina, this happens all the time with children. Maya is trying out her new independence and she sees her separation from you very differently than she used to. Now she knows you are gone when you go. She may be telling you she is confused, mad, and, just maybe, that she wants you to spend some time with her playing in her space before you go home." Marina thought about this, looked intently into Maya's eyes, and said in a soft voice: "Maya, do you want Mama to play with you?" Maya, with bright eyes, repeated "Mama play? Mama play"?

Shanita, knowing how different infants work through the strong emotions associated with their emerging understanding of people and objects, intervenes quickly by telling the mother that what is happening is normal and does not mean that the baby now prefers her caregiver to her mother. By doing so, she avoids the development of jealousy that might undermine her relationship with Marina. By "talking through the baby," Shanita offers Marina several ways to understand Maya's behavior and some strategies the two of them can use to work through the transition together. The alliance is saved. Shanita is using her knowledge and skills to help both mother and baby are negotiate what will be one of many emotionally charged moments.

● ● ● ● ●
Toddlers *(16 to 36 months)*
● ● ● ● ●

Toddlers are concerned about who they are and who is in charge. Beginning around 18 months of age, identity becomes the dominant developmental issue for children, closely tied to questions of independence and control. Of course, the sense of security that began to develop in the earliest months and the desire to explore (with increasing purposefulness) continue. Caregivers can help toddlers find appropriate ways to assert themselves by supporting their individuality, by giving them choices whenever possible, and by introducing social guidelines. A well-designed environment that offers toddlers chances to be in control, and to participate in group play, fantasy play and independent activity helps the caregiver to foster cooperation and facilitate the toddler's development of a strong sense of self.

● The child

Toddlers are learning how to be safe, how to get what they need without taking from others, how to use peers and adults as resources, how to use words to express feelings, and how to act appropriately in different situations. They have a heightened interest in what it is to be a boy or a girl. They are particularly interested in their bodies and those of others. Toddlers' interactions may at times seem very sophisticated (as, for example, when they imitate a gentle, patient, or generous adult). At other times, fatigue, anxiety, or other distress overwhelms them.

The period from 16 to 36 months is filled with exploration, questioning, discovery, and determina-

tion to find meaning in events, objects, and words. Through their experimentation with objects, language, and social interactions, toddlers are entering a new phase of mental activity. Toddlers love to divide objects into categories by shape, size, color or type. They might line up all the large rubber animals according to their height, put the animals into groups according to their species, and pair a little animal next to a big one calling them "mommy and baby." They are demonstrating through their play their rudimentary understanding of classification and seriation. What they are learning through play, observation, and exploration is often amazing. For example, while reading a story, a toddler might point to all the cats in a picture, calling them "cats" even though they are different sizes, shapes and colors.

Toddlers are fascinated by the use of words. Words are new tools for relating to peers and adults. They listen and can follow simple instructions. They ask "why" repeatedly in order to engage adults as much as to get answers. Words have power. Toddlers can use words to evoke what is not present and to express strong feelings. For example, they often repeat phrases like "mommy come back" in a ritualistic way to comfort themselves when feeling the sadness of separation, and to reassure themselves that the separation is not permanent.

Toddlers who have watched adults and older sibling write, who are read to from books, and who see printed words used to label objects on shelves or names printed on their cubbies become increasingly aware of the importance of written language. Not only do they enjoy being read to, they are more attentive to the words on the page. They label the things they see in illustrations and often join in the telling of the story. As with spoken language, toddlers use their keen powers of observation and desire to imitate the activities of adults and older children around them to learn about various forms of written language before they can read or write.

The social awareness of toddlers is vastly more complex than that of younger infants. Their past experiences in communicating with others enable them to refine their ability to read children's and adults' signals. They demonstrate their growing familiarity with symbols through their dramatic play and their rapidly expanding vocabularies. They are now interested in playing with each other. As they play, toddlers learn from other children's actions and experience the power of "teaching" and guiding others in play. Using their few words, gestural language, and boundless creativity, they can work out simple dramatic play themes like pretending that a block is a telephone, dressing up to dance, or carrying a briefcase to "go to work."

Toddlers' exploration of the social world often involves conflict. The most basic is about what is mine and what is yours. Toddlers react impulsively, but their feelings of empathy blossom as they negotiate these conflicts and see that other people have feelings too. They can easily fall into despair at not getting what they want or feeling the displeasure of a beloved adult; just as easily, they can react with amazing generosity and warmth. Through such negotiations, toddlers build a sense of themselves as social beings—competent, cooperative, and emotionally connected.

● The caregiver

The skilled caregiver offers toddlers experiences that support initiative, creativity, autonomy, and self-esteem. Yet she recognizes that while striving to be independent and self-reliant, toddlers count on the understanding and vigilance of the adults who love them. The caregiver must be prepared to

Donna positioned Haniya, a toddler with cerebral palsy, in her special seat on the countertop, so that Haniya could hold her hands under the faucet. Jonathan came in from the adjoining play area to wash his hands before snack. Donna said to Jonathan, "Please turn on the faucet for Haniya." Jonathan did. Haniya glanced at him and gave a faint smile. She stuck her hands under the faucet of running water, seeming to enjoy the cool feeling on her hands. Jonathan stuck his hands under the water also and they splashed the water together. Haniya's smile filled her face and they laughed. Jonathan pushed the soap dispenser for Haniya then for himself. Donna helped both children wash between their fingers then gave Haniya a paper towel to give Jonathan, who took it gently from her saying "tank you, Hanya."

This caregiver knows how to extend this moment of intimacy and cooperation between these two toddlers, letting each use his skills to help the other. She only intervenes to be sure that each child learns proper hand washing. Thus, good habits of personal hygiene, essential for reducing the spread of infection in child care settings, are taught within the context of interaction and cooperation. The bathroom is also set up to offer such opportunities, with a place to sit for the child who needs to be held and a stool for the child who can stand. It allows both children to reach the sink, soap and paper towels on their own. Teaching proper personal hygiene is critical as toddlers are increasingly capable of doing things by themselves and learning to use the toilet. What could be better than the magic of one toddler helping another and showing off new competence at proper hand washing?

prevent injuries and handle conflicts as toddlers learn to defend themselves, share, and cooperate with others. The competent caregiver knows that her toddlers are capable and want to test their social skills. She gives them opportunities to "take responsibility" for others, and takes advantage of unplanned encounters that allow the toddler to show his competence.

Toddlers need opportunities to be responsible, to make significant choices, and to be challenged or disciplined in ways that keep their dignity intact. They are beginning to understand why certain behaviors must be limited —— that rules are fair and judgments just. They need to feel that limits are placed on them by adults who can be counted on and who mean what they say. These are adults who can support them in their frustrations and disappointments and enjoy their pleasures and successes. Toddlers need continuity between the expectations of their family and those of their caregiver. Toddlers can cope with the fact that rules about what is acceptable or unacceptable differ between home and the child care setting, but caregivers and parents must work together to make these differences clear to children.

Adults can expect great variability in emotion and social interaction and learn when to let toddlers work a conflict through themselves and when to intervene. Adults who know a toddler well can recognize the signs of stress and help the child learn to control her impulses; they also know when a toddler is acting out deep emotions and give him the space to work them through.

Unfortunately, many infants and toddlers experience the trauma of fighting in the family, divorce, chronic illness, death of a family member or violence in the community. Their ability to overcome the hurt and fear depends, in large measure, on whether they are secure in relationships with a few caring adults who understand what they have ex-

During a walk in the park, Richie picked up a large branch that had fallen from a tree. As Amy began her customary speech about leaving sticks on the ground because they might poke someone, Richie explained that the stick was his cello. He ran his hand across the branch singing "de—dah," tapping his toes and moving his head to the beat. "OK," Amy said, "we'll take the cello back with us." Richie's father, a musician, had recently moved out of the house. Amy thought that music was a connection with his father. When the group got back to the center, Richie, sitting on a milk crate and using a wooden spoon for a bow, gave the group a concert with his cello. It was the beginning of a ritual. Every afternoon after nap, children would help get the cello out from under the red sofa, and there would be a concert as Richie created a connection with his father.

In a few critical minutes during an ordinary outing, this caregiver draws on many areas of knowledge, skill, and experience. As Richie picks up a stick, Amy's practiced vigilance about children's safety and health lead her to intervene quickly. But as Richie explains (his experience with Amy must have taught him that she will listen), Amy slows down. Her general knowledge of toddler development helps her to appreciate Richie's emerging capacities to express himself through language and dramatic play. Her awareness of Richie's specific situation helps her to grasp the emotional meaning of "the cello" for Richie and to find a way to support this young child's courageous effort to maintain connection with his father. Amy adapts rapidly. She agrees to carry the stick—protecting, simultaneously, the group's safety, the group's respect for safety rules, Richie's dignity, and her individual relationship of trust with Richie. Once back at the center, Amy creates an opportunity for Richie to use his creativity not only to master his own pain but also to contribute to the shared life of the group. We can imagine that in conversations with Richie's mother and father, Amy will listen for opportunities to let each of them know about the cello concerts and then listen carefully for clues to help her support the whole family during this difficult transition.

perienced and give them extra attention, tolerance, and appreciation for how they express their feelings. Often, the caregiver grieves with the child. The caregiver's greatest assets in dealing with such situations are her responsiveness to the child and her commitment to being a resource to the family.

The caregiver/family alliance

A healthy toddler's inner world is filled with conflicting feelings ——independence and dependence, pride and shame, confidence and doubt, self-awareness and confusion, fear and omnipotence, hostility and intense love, anger and tenderness, initiative and passivity. These feelings challenge parents' and caregivers' resourcefulness and knowledge, as they work together to provide toddlers with emotional security.

A child's sense of identity is rooted in his family and community. Toddlers feel more secure when they can see that their family members are comfortable with their caregivers. Family-caregiver communication, particularly when there are cultural and language differences, builds mutual understanding and creates continuity between home and child care. If the family child care provider or child care center staff do not know the home language of the child, there are strategies available to meet the challenge. For example, bilingual, bicultural members of the family's community can be recruited to interpret during family-caregiver conferences, interpret important program policies and help the caregiver learn at least a few important words. There are many ways to show respect and help the family feel welcome in the child care setting.

Toddlers whose home language is different from that used in the group care environment need to hear their own language spoken and see it written.

With Ben, the course of toilet learning was not entirely smooth, though not really difficult. When Ben was 19 months old and his father raised the issue with Carla, Ben's primary caregiver, they agreed to start a toilet routine both at home and at the center. At the center, Carla began suggesting that Ben might like to go to the toilet. When he agreed, they would go to the bathroom together. She would remove his diaper and let him step on the small platform to sit on the toilet. The first day, he wet himself as his diaper was being removed. However, on the second day, he had a bowel movement on the toilet and seemed very pleased with himself. For the next few days, he would occasionally urinate or defecate in the toilet with some pleasure. Then Ben entered a period when he wasn't sure the whole thing was a good idea. At 20 $1/2$ months, when asked to go to the toilet, he answered vehemently, "No!" Carla talked to Ben's father, who described the same resistance at home, and they decided not to press him for a while. A few weeks later, Ben's father told Carla that Ben tried to show his baby brother the toilet and suggested this might be a signal. Why not try asking Ben to take a friend to the toilet? Ben seemed eager, and Carla listened as he talked convincingly about toilets and sinks and how they weren't bad. He was still reluctant for short periods of time, and his father and Carla would suggest "helping a friend," which usually worked. By 26 months of age, Ben was using the toilet willingly, standing to urinate; he wore a diaper only at nap time. Soon after that, he either went to the bathroom himself or asked to be taken. He remained a good helper to his friends and was particularly skilled as a handwashing instructor.

The primary caregiver follows the cues of the child and the family, continually encouraging toilet learning through reminders, actual trips to the toilet, and praise, but without punishment or shaming when expectations are not met. The staff also recognizes in Ben's behavior typical struggles that happen during toilet learning: The child wishes both to learn and not to learn to use the toilet; may be temporarily scared, seeing something that comes from him go away so fast and so permanently; or may not be ready to control his bowels. Talking and sharing observations of Ben helped both father and caregiver know when it might be time to try again and how they might approach toilet learning. For Ben, the chance to be "responsible" for a friend was the key to overcoming his reluctance.

These opportunities help them build upon their home language while learning words to communicate with English-speaking peers and caregivers. In valuing the child's home language, caregivers reinforce his pride in family and community as well as his feelings of competence in mastering the challenges of a culturally and linguistically different environment.

Bowel control and learning to use the toilet are important issues during the third year of life. Toilet learning can only be effective if the child wants to learn and feels responsible. It must be accomplished in a spirit of cooperation and enthusiasm as children reach this milestone in their development. Professionals must ensure that common, but inappropriate, techniques, such as punishment or shaming children, are not used in the child care setting. The family and caregiver should agree upon an approach for helping the older toddler learn this new aspect of self-control.

Caring for toddlers can be challenging for adults. The toddler's constant movement, short attention span, and bouts of frustration mixed with the pure joy of discovery can be both heart-warming and emotionally draining. It is difficult at times to understand that as he pushes away and hurdles himself into action, the toddler is still very much in need of his special adults and the secure base they offer. Parents and caregivers who have built a good relationship can help each other better understand and help the toddler as they share their experiences and insights and offer each other encouragement.

SECTION II

Components of Quality Infant/toddler Child Care

IN ORDER TO ACHIEVE QUALITY infant/toddler child care, eight components of early group experience must be addressed:

1. health and safety;

2. small groups for infants and toddlers, with high staff-to-child ratios;

3. primary caregiver assignments;

4. continuity of care;

5. responsive caregiving/planning;

6. cultural and linguistic continuity;

7. meeting the needs of the individual within the group context; and

8. the physical environment.

Understanding these components and translating them into daily practice require on-going opportunities for staff training, supervision and mentorship.

● 1. Promoting health and safety

Infants and toddlers are more susceptible than older children to infectious disease because their immune systems have not fully developed. In addition, their emerging mobility and curiosity put them at increased risk of injury. A basic challenge in the group care of infants and toddlers is creating a safe and sanitary environment that is interesting to the children and can be maintained efficiently so that caregivers have enough time for intimate, responsive interaction with each infant and toddler. Achieving efficient health and safety policies and procedures requires:

a. careful planning of areas for food preparation and diapering/toileting, including adequate storage cabinets easily accessible to adults ;

b. detailed and scrupulously maintained health policies, emergency, injury and health procedures, and child and staff health records, including health and injury reports;

c. policies and procedures that are concise but thorough and designed for the most efficient use of staff time;

d. orientation, in-service training, and ongoing supervision specifically on handwashing, sanitation, the proper handling and storage of disinfectants, and use of gloves;

e. time for caregivers to meet to share current health/safety information, concerns, and problems and generate solutions;

f. daily communication between family members and caregivers, with daily record-keeping on each infant/toddler and special reports to all families when an infectious disease is present or a safety issue (including lead poisoning hazards in the community) has arisen;

g. vigilant monitoring procedures for health and safety; and

h. knowledge of and collaboration with community health and safety resources.

Every caregiver should be trained in pediatric first aid and rescue breathing. Because getting infants and toddlers out of a building is complicated (with their extra clothes, emergency information, diapers, etc.), emergency evacuation procedures must be planned carefully and practiced regularly. Family child care providers and center directors must write and maintain records on children's immunizations and physical examinations, incidents of infectious disease or injury, staff immunization histories and annual physicals (including the Mantau T.B. test). Caregivers should be alerted to, and shown ways to minimize, the most common health hazards of their occupation, such as back injuries resulting from lifting infants and toddlers.

Caregivers should be aware of and know how to use the health resources that are available in their

"I love my babies, but I must have changed 100 diapers and I feel that all I do is wipe bottoms and noses all day!" All the infant caregivers nodded as Sonja spoke. Dora, the infant/toddler program director, had planned a meeting on using caregiving routines as a special time for infant and caregiver to have some private time, but she appreciated Sonja's feelings and forthrightness in expressing them. Instead of her planned agenda, Dora decided to send her infant/toddler staff, in teams of three, to inventory and evaluate their diaper-changing areas. The reports resulted in a long list of problems to prioritize and resolve, including: caregivers needed to reach for too many things before diapering; getting plastic gloves on and off was a hassle—it seemed impossible to avoid contaminating their hands, the baby or supplies either before or as they were getting the gloves off; the diaper area lacked wall displays a baby would enjoy looking at or touching; the disinfectant bottle was left out too often because there was no easy-to-reach, secure place for it.

In a medical facility, it would be unthinkable not to train and monitor staff sanitary practices like handwashing, putting on and taking off protective gloves, using elbow faucets, and disposing of contaminated materials. Such training is equally important in group child care. The use of protective gloves for diapering and cleaning blood or body fluids is a good example. If caregivers are not trained and monitored in the correct use of plastic gloves, the chances of spreading germs and bacteria are increased. Health and safety training should be part of orientation for all new staff and reinforced by strong policies and procedures, visual reminders, supervision, and regular training sessions.

community. Families often need help identifying a primary health provider and keeping current with immunizations and well-baby check-ups. Given the low wages and benefits typical in the child care field, caregivers must be resourceful in order to find good health care for themselves and keep a healthy regimen. Experienced caregivers who have resource information to offer, translated into families' home language if required, can help children and families get the ongoing health supervision they need.

Any child care setting will benefit from a health consultant (for example, a visiting health nurse or local pediatrician) to advise on potential infectious diseases, explain symptoms and treatments to families, plan health alert procedures when infectious disease occurs, and assist with public health reporting requirements. Environmental health specialists, playground designers, and other professionals can offer expertise on outdoor and indoor equipment safety, traffic and fire safety. A mental health consultant can be invaluable in helping staff to foster the healthy social and emotional development of children and families while also protecting their own emotional well-being.

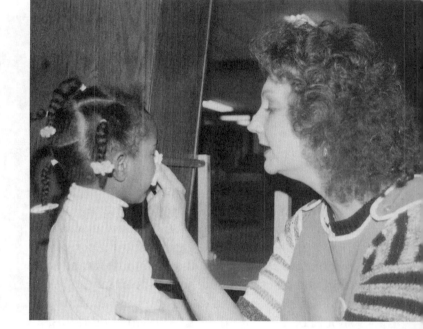

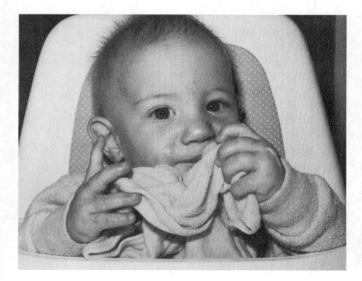

2. Serving infants and toddlers in small groups with high staff-to-child ratios

Group size and adult-to-child ratios are both important. Empirical research and the wisdom of early care specialists have consistently identified these two indicators as critical to quality child care. No more than six children who are not yet mobile should be in a group; a caregiver should be responsible for no more than three young infants. No more than nine children who are crawling (up to 18 months) should be in a group, with a caregiver responsible for no more than 3 mobile infants (explorers are active and need a watchful eye). For children 18 months to three years, group size should be no more than 12, staff-to-child ratios, 1:4. Centers, group homes, and family child care homes with mixed age groupings should never have more than two children under two years of age in a single group.

The amount of space needed per child is grossly underestimated in many state licensing rules. A standard for quality should specify 350 square feet per group of six infants; 500 square feet for 9 mobile infants; and 600 square feet for a group of 12 toddlers.

Small groups create a sense of intimacy and safety. The rich dialogue between caregivers and infants that is carried out through gesture, vocalization, and eye contact is possible in small groups because there are fewer bodies, less noise, and less activity to interfere. With high staff-to-child ratios and small groups, caregivers can build strong relationships with individual children and adapt activities and arrange furniture and equipment to meet the changing interests and capacities of the group. It is easier to know the families. With fewer distractions and less noise, adults can talk comfort-

After moving from the intimacy of the infant room to the big room with its high ceilings, high windows, and four groups of 12 toddlers (18 to 36 months of age) sharing the same space, Kim's group of toddlers seemed to "fall apart." Emmanuel (25 months), in particular, was always in trouble and had started biting. Emmanuel's parents were also upset because he was irritable and tired at the end of the day and aggressive with his cousins on the weekends. Kim talked about him with her colleagues in the toddler program. It seemed that everyone was having discipline problems. The caregivers were all feeling irritable and unhappy with how they were with their children. They made a "wish list" to give to the center director, parents, and members of the center's board of directors. First on their list was partitions, made of solid material from the floor to a height of five feet and soundproof plexiglass to the ceiling. Second was creating two open spaces for art and other messy activities and active indoor play; these would be shared by the groups of toddlers. The list also included ideas to consider: dropping the ceilings and adding acoustical ceiling tiles; installing lower lights for a softer effect; and building lofts so children could get away from the group and look out the windows. The caregivers knew that creating an intimate environment would require a substantial investment, but they were ready to join with families and the board of directors to identify resources in the community and funds from state and local government or private sources.

The movement of too many bodies doing too many different things, the glare of bright overhead lights, and unrelentingly high noise levels take their toll on children and adults. In a large group, a fast-moving toddler like Emmanuel will find it very difficult to learn boundaries—where to stop so you don't disrupt, how loud to talk, how to get attention, how to protect what's yours from the intrusion of other fast-moving peers. Kim can help Emmanuel by charting a safe course of activities and anticipating his frustration because she knows him, but her resources are limited, and the challenges are enormous.

In a small infant group, eye contact or a gesture would be enough to stop Emmanuel and direct him away from trouble; now she must yell or get to him before something happens. In the infant room, he explored his environment freely, returning to her or glancing at her for reassurance. In the larger space with so many other children and adults, he no longer knows the rules and can't see her easily. Because Kim can't see Emmanuel easily, she can't react promptly to his subtle cues.

ably. This is critical to building trusting relationships, understanding and adapting to children with special needs, and appreciating cultural and linguistic differences.

All infants and toddlers need individualized, responsive, and respectful care. High staff-to-child ratios and small groups make this possible. High staff-to-child ratios and small groups are essential to meet the needs of infants and toddlers with chronic illnesses or disabilities in inclusive settings.

3. Primary caregiver assignments

The assignment of a primary caregiver to every child in group care means that when a child first enters child care, family members know the person who is principally responsible for their child. Primary caregiving in a center or large family group care setting does not mean that one person cares for an infant or toddler exclusively, all of the time—there has to be team work. Primary caregiving does mean that the infant or toddler and his family have someone special with whom to build an intimate relationship. A policy of primary caregiver assignments is strong evidence that a child care program takes seriously the importance of continuing, positive, intimate relationships. Primary caregiving is essential to a child care program philosophy that values relationships. It is a statement to families that relationships are the key to quality caregiving.

A primary caregiver can use an infant or toddler's entry into child care to teach memorable lessons—for example: "Those I love leave and come back; they make sure I am safe while they are away; they spend time in this place where I play, and are comfortable with this new person who cares for me. I can trust this new person because my parents like her and spend time with her.

This is a safe place to be." When a primary caregiver and family members spend time together, they build the foundations of a trusting working relationship. Regular communication will offer invaluable opportunities for mutual reassurance and support, as parents and caregiver anticipate and cope with the normal challenges of early development and the needs and interests of the individual child.

4. Continuity of care

Having one primary caregiver for more than a year (optimally, from entry into child care until the child is three years of age or older) is important to the infant's emotional development. Switching from one caregiver to another (which in some programs occurs as often as every six to nine months) takes its toll. When a very young child loses a caregiver, he loses part of his sense of himself and of how the world operates—the things that the child knows how to do, and the ways that he knows to be, simply don't work any more. Too many changes in caregivers can lead to a child's reluctance to form new relationships.

Continuity of care—or the lack of it—in a program has important implications for the entire group of children. A child with a new caregiver has to work hard to get her messages across. The caregiver can only guess at what she wants. There is confusion and stress for both child and caregiver. If a child deals with change by acting out her frustration, this will have an impact on the entire group. With a caregiver who knows her, however, a child can express her needs less dramatically. The better somebody knows a child, the more easily she will understand the subtle cues that reveal what the child needs.

Continuity of care is important for caregivers

Before Tyrone began full-time child care, his parents met with the director of the center and with Beth, the woman who would be Tyrone's primary caregiver. The center's policy encouraged such family visits and meetings. Tyrone's parents described their 11-month-old son as sensitive and slow to warm up to new people. They also said he was expressing fear when they went out or were not in sight. The director responded that the transition into child care might go more smoothly if the family, Tyrone, and Beth could spend extra time together. Beth asked how much time each parent could spend at the center in the first month of transition, and they worked out a schedule for spending whole days, then part days, then visits, before leaving Tyrone at the center all day. During this time, Tyrone and his parents not only became comfortable with Beth, but also with Emma and Spencer (the other two infants for whom Beth was primary caregiver) and their families.

The initial transition into the child care setting, morning arrivals and evening departures while the infant or toddler is in care, and the transition out of the child care setting are all critical experiences. Many families may find these transitions difficult. Taking time from work to stay with the infant or toddler who is beginning child care, spending time in the morning, and leaving work with enough time and energy for a relaxed reunion in the evening are all challenges. Acknowledging the stress that families experience, caregivers must be strong enough in their convictions about the importance of relationship-building, trust, and information-sharing to work with each family to create a schedule that will work for them.

and parents as well as for children. When infants and toddlers are moved to a new room as they reach a new developmental stage, caregivers don't get to see the fruition of their work. Parents who have developed trust in their child's first primary caregiver—often a slow process—have to build trust all over again with a new caregiver.

The staff turn-over rate in child care is currently so high that it is hard to imagine meeting the goal of continuity-of-caregiver for every child birth to three. This goal is too important, however, not to strive for it. Infant/toddler caregivers can be trained and encouraged to move with their infants, taking on an additional child as their infants move into toddlerhood. Alternately, infant/toddler areas can be designed for flexibility, so that group sizes and staff-child ratios can be expanded, furniture can be reorganized to define activity areas, and more complex play materials can be introduced to challenge increasing skills and wider interests as babies become mobile infants and then toddlers.

5. Responsive caregiving/ planning

Watching, asking, and adapting are the tools of responsive caregiving. Responsive group care for children throughout the infant/toddler years (and beyond) involves knowing each child and taking cues from the child and the group about when to expand on the child's initiative, when to guide, when to teach, when to intervene—and when to watch, wait, and applaud a child's efforts and eventual success. Responsive caregiving involves using daily caregiving routines and plans flexibly, adapting them to the moods, interests, and needs of the individual child and of the group as a whole.

The freedom to make choices and to experience the world on their own terms encourages young

Isa had several different caregivers before joining Hanna's group at 12 months. It took time and the joint efforts of Aisha, Isa's single mother, and Hanna for Isa to feel secure in her new child care setting. In the first days, Isa learned the name—Abbie—of one of the toddlers, who had been with Hanna since she was 6 months old. Isa and Abbie's interest in each other was reassuring to both Hanna and Aisha. They talked about ways to use this blossoming friendship to help with the transition. Abbie's trust and love of Hanna seemed to help Isa want to be close as well. Within weeks, Isa was thriving, and the friendship between Isa and Abbie had extended to their respective families.

In addition to the friendship between Abbie and Isa, there were other things about Hanna and the child care center in which she worked that helped Isa overcome her fear of getting close to another strange adult. Hanna valued relationships and understood Isa's feelings. She encouraged Aisha to call Isa during the day. She also gathered information about Isa's home life and asked Aisha to help her incorporate into Isa's day at the center words, music, a special blanket, pictures, routines and anything else familiar that would help establish continuity between her home and center. Hanna knew that Isa would feel safer if she saw that her mother was comfortable at the center. Hanna had established close relationships of long standing with her other two babies and their families. In the mornings and evenings, the adults chatted and played with the children like friends getting together. Hanna encouraged Aisha to spend time at the center also, and with a little encouragement, Aisha became comfortable with the other family members.

children's sense of themselves as competent learners, socially adept communicators, and successful problem-solvers. Close, continuing, and mutually pleasurable relationships between caregivers and children make this kind of learning possible.

Responsive caregiving and planning, for both the individual child and the group, involve more than planning cognitively focused games and activities. The responsive caregiver has an overall plan for each day, including materials and activities that are appropriate for the developmental stage of the group. In addition, the caregiver continually observes each infant or toddler to discover what skills he is ready to explore and eventually master. Within a safe environment, the responsive caregiver provides a thoughtful variety of toys matched to the infant's interests and skills. She gives the young child uninterrupted time to explore and helps her to cope and persevere when frustrated. She uses language to label objects, sounds, and feelings. She guides the infant's interactions with others.

6. Cultural, linguistic, and familial continuity

Child rearing reflects the values and beliefs of families and the culture of their community. The most basic acts of caring—feeding, comforting, toileting, playing—reflect the caregiver's values. These, in turn, reflect the caregiver's own childhood experiences, her training as a child care provider, and other cultural influences. Therefore, self-reflection is the first step toward offering culturally sensitive care. Caregiver training and on-going supervision should emphasize this key skill. By exploring their own backgrounds, caregivers can learn to see the roots of some of their most basic child care beliefs and practices. Feedings are a good example. A

Clarissa (11 months) was in her high chair while Brian, her primary caregiver, sat in front of her feeding Joey (8 months) his bottle. Brian was not comfortable with the mess Clarissa was making—squashing pieces of banana, dropping bits she failed to get into her mouth, and getting banana on everything within her reach. She was making a real mess! However, he was enjoying her enthusiasm and her increasing skills too much to interfere. Instead, he got a sturdy bowl, put the banana in it, and offered Clarissa a spoon. She accepted the challenge. To Brian's relief, the banana pieces stayed in the bowl and Clarissa's hands focused on the spoon rather than exploring the surfaces around her. Brian was tempted to intervene again as she struggled to get the banana on the spoon and make it stay there while she tried to find her mouth with the spoon and get it in. He wanted to hold Clarissa's hand so that she would know how it felt to get it right (and get some banana at the same time). But observing Clarissa's intensity and resourcefulness, Brian held back. It would take some time for Clarissa to learn to handle the spoon and slippery food, he realized, but when she succeeded, the achievement would be her very own.

Rather than trying to teach a very young child a specific skill, Brian focuses on facilitating infants' and toddlers' natural interests and urges to learn. When a caregiver trusts that infants learn through this responsive approach, he allows infants and toddlers the full benefit of exploration and problem-solving, as well as the rewards of mastery. Such experiences build confidence in conquering new challenges. Knowing when to step back is as important as knowing when and how to intervene.

caregiver raised to feel that independence and early mastery of skills are important may see mealtimes as an opportunity to strengthen children's small motor skills and hand-eye coordination by encouraging self-feeding. In contrast, a caregiver who grew up in a culture where the availability of food was a concern may want to convey the message that food must never be wasted; she is likely to want to control how the infant eats. Caregivers must recognize their own values and understand that they are being transmitted to the children.

Reflecting on their backgrounds, their beliefs, and their reasons for choosing the work they do will help caregivers to be honest with themselves and with families. It is not helpful to pretend to be interested in the parent's point of view. Rather, caregivers must uncover the values that underlie their own beliefs, become aware of multiple perspectives on child rearing, be open to the parent's point of view when there are differences, and be willing to change some of their practices.

Caregivers who use the infant's home language reinforce the infant's sense of "rightness" and sense of belonging in both the home and child care environment. Speaking the child's home language, welcoming family members into the child care setting, and respecting the child-rearing values and beliefs of the child's family all support the early development of a strong sense of identity. To provide cultural and familial continuity, infant/toddler child care programs should, when possible, employ staff who are of the same culture and who speak the same language as the children served. If this is not possible, asking family members to volunteer or recruiting volunteers from the community can prevent barriers and open communication.

Open communication among parents, and between families and child care directors, is as essential as communication between families and their child's primary caregiver. Families should be in-

Miguel's father confided to Yolanda that he was worried when he saw his 26-month-old son playing at cooking and housecleaning in the house corner. Yolanda promised to bring the issue up at staff meeting, and did so. She restated the center's philosophy regarding valuing cultural and linguistic differences. Some staff saw conflict between respecting cultural values and tolerating sexism. Yolanda redirected her staff's attention to two questions: 1) Why were possible dramatic play themes limited to what goes on in a house? and 2) What did they know about Miguel's culture, family and community that could be brought into the dramatic play area? The discussion that followed revealed that many of her staff wanted larger, more flexible, and more varied props for their children's dramatic play. The meeting turned to brainstorming, and staff generated a long list of ideas for making prop boxes, assembling a variety of clothing, and encouraging a range of dramatic play themes. Finally, Yolanda asked them to think of ways that Miguel's father and other families could be recruited to help.

The director set the tone for the discussion, quickly intervening when she perceived her staff responding defensively. She effectively guided them into thinking about what children learn in dramatic play and how they use what they know from home and community. Solutions then flowed from the staff, not from the director. Yolanda was responsive to the family's concerns and respectful of her staff. Reflection, observation, and collaborative problem-solving helped everyone learn more about both dramatic play and culture. She also involved Miguel's father to help identify the best solutions and locate the materials they would need. She invited staff to involve other families as a way to stress that family member concerns were appreciated and their ideas were valued.

vited to share in program planning and encouraged to communicate their concerns and their ideas. Gentle but persistent encouragement may be necessary for families from cultures in which refraining from comment is a sign of respect for the caregiver's authority. When parents do have concerns, they should be encouraged to express them and be part of the problem-solving process.

A careful survey of program policies and practices, physical environment, and materials is the first step to making them reflect the cultural, linguistic and ethnic diversity of children's families. The survey asks two basic questions about each aspect of caregiving: 1) Does this help each child and adult feel their culture and language are valued? and 2), if not, what can be changed to reflect home cultures and languages in the child care setting?

7. Meeting the needs of the individual within the group context

Infants are individuals. They differ from each other in many ways—biological rhythms, rates of development, and behavior that reflects primary cultural, linguistic, and child-rearing experiences at home. Attention to other components of quality infant/toddler care—health and safety, group sizes and staff-child ratios, primary caregiver assignments, continuity of care, cultural and familial continuity, responsive caregiving/planning, and the physical environment—makes it possible to meet the needs of the individual infant or toddler within a group context. Appreciating the uniqueness of each infant, observing him over time, learning his preferences and moods, and understanding his needs reward the caregiver and enrich the experience of group care for the child and family.

In an intimate setting, flexible scheduling is pos-

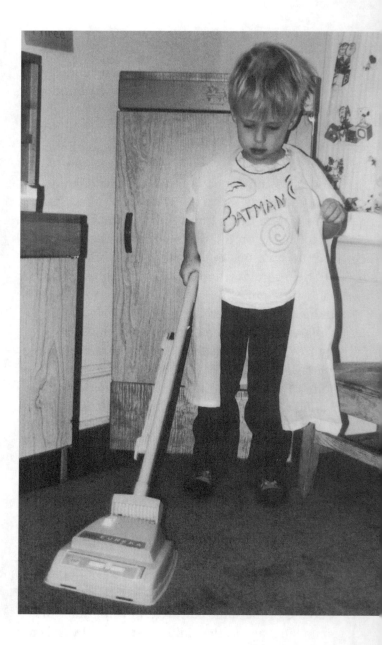

sible. Babies sleep when they want to sleep. They eat when they are hungry, and are fed with food that meets their individual needs. Infants and toddlers can play when they want to play, with plenty of opportunities to explore a variety of toys and materials, and to play alone, with other children, and with adults. Since babies' rhythms are individual, a caregiver can expect that one of her infants could be sleeping, while another is absorbed in quiet play, while she is actively engaging a third. An intimate setting recognizes mobile infants' and toddlers' individual needs to explore, assert autonomy, and periodically reconnect with the secure base their caregiver provides.

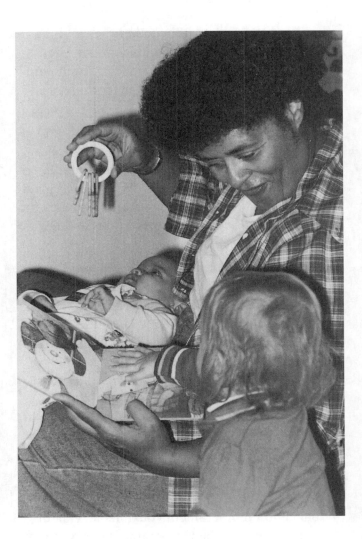

Families will readily share how different one child is from another. Caregivers observe differences among even the very youngest babies in their care, describing babies as "quiet," "easygoing," or "active." Researchers describe people's characteristic styles of reacting and responding as temperament. Caregivers will recognize three temperament types that characterize many infants and toddlers:

• A **flexible child** is generally open to new people and experiences, is not alarmed by sudden occurrences, and adapts quickly to what is going on.

• A **feisty child** is energetic, active, and can appear more demanding.

• A **fearful child**, by contrast, may appear shy and easily alarmed. These children like to take their time in approaching new people, activities or objects.

Understanding the concept of temperament is critical to handling individual differences appropriately in the context of group care. Several points are important to remember :

• Differences in temperament, even at the extremes, are differences in the normal range of behavior. To be flexible, feisty or fearful in temperament has little to do with whether the child is able to learn, develop strong relationships, and get along with others. Recognizing a child's temperamental characteristics is important for responsive caregiving.

• A supportive caregiver who understands and accepts a child's temperamental characteristics can, over time, help a feisty or fearful child handle potentially distressing situations. With the caregiver's help these can become valuable opportunities for the child to master social expectations and develop confidence and self-worth.

• Any temperamental trait can be an asset or a liability. How parents and caregivers respond to the child's temperament can play a big role in the child's emotional development, since the feedback that the child gets from adults contributes to the self-image the child develops.

• Caregivers need to be aware of their own responses to children with different temperaments. A feisty child might irritate one adult but be challenging and exciting to another. Some caregivers may find certain temperamental traits difficult to understand.

• Caregivers need to be aware not only of the individual child's temperament (flexible, fearful, or feisty), but also of the temperamental mix of any group of children and caregivers.

Fortunately, child care of all kinds is becoming "inclusive" by opening its doors to infants and toddlers with special needs. Providing developmentally appropriate group care for infants and toddlers with special needs may involve careful supervision of daily routines (e.g., for children with severe allergies), availability of medically necessary devices (e.g., oxygen tents for children with severe asthma, apnea monitors for infants at risk for SIDS), and practice in the use of assistive technology (e.g., augmentative communication and pow-

Peg (22 months) started to bite other children. Aisha, her primary caregiver, observed Peg carefully and asked her parents and grandparents to do the same. They all agreed on words to use with Peg about biting and about how to treat her when she did bite. Aisha asked Peg's family whether anything had changed at home, with relatives, or whether some event in the community might be making Peg anxious. After a few weeks (and several meetings with families whose toddlers had been bitten by Peg), family and child care staff did not know what more to do. Aisha asked the family to think about asking an infant mental health specialist from the child care consultation service at the children's hospital to observe Peg at the center. Peg's family had seen Kadija, a clinical psychologist, before, since she often came to the center to consult with caregivers and facilitate workshops and discussions with parents. The family agreed, and Kadija came to the center to observe Peg. After several observations, Kadija met with the family and Aisha. She confirmed what they had already observed about Peg—that she tends to be frightened easily, reserved with new people and activities, and very focused when she works. Kadija said she had observed Peg react with alarm when she was interrupted while playing by her-

self and when she was crowded or bumped by other toddlers. "Watch Peg's expression," Kadija said, "and intervene whenever her eyes get big and round and her mouth opens. Try to help her find ways to protect herself by telling her to get her special carpet square or a tray to put her things on. Give her some simple phrases like "no touch" and "Peg's place," and talk to the other children to let them know what she means. If Peg bites, tell her she must hold on to a part of your clothing. Then look at her firmly and say, "No biting." As Peg holds onto you, soothe the bitten toddler. Ask Peg to do what you do when she feels like helping her friend feel better."

A professional who is trained to observe and interpret young children's behavior, play, and interactions with people and things can be a tremendous resource to caregivers and families. Understanding the meaning of an infant or toddler's withdrawn, challenging, or disruptive behavior helps the caregiver and family devise approaches that will work for the individual child and the whole group. Providing specialized support to infants, toddlers, their families, and caregivers within the child care setting can be a wise investment of scarce community mental health resources.

Caregivers are in a unique position to help guide families to assessment, diagnostic and treatment services because they see both family member and child every day, and they share a common goal—to support the child's healthy development.

ered mobility devices). Group care also offers opportunities to promote the healthy development of infants and toddlers with, or at risk of, emotional or behavioral disorders.

Children with special needs are children first. Caregivers' wide experience of variations in developmental patterns and their ability to observe individual children closely over time and in a range of situations make them invaluable partners in the process of identifying and evaluating infants' and toddlers' developmental problems, and in planning and implementing strategies to foster optimal development. The caregiver adapts her caregiving to the child with special needs in the same way she would to meet the individual needs and interests of any other child.

8. The environment

The physical environment—indoors and out—can promote or impede intimate, satisfying relationships. It takes a great deal of planning and ongoing evaluation and improvement to create spaces for infants, toddlers, caregivers, and their families that meet the needs of each.

Spaces must be constructed for efficiency, so that routine management is done effectively but quickly. Spaces must provide growing infants with a wide variety of interesting objects, textures and physical challenges, while neither overwhelming them with choices nor jeopardizing their safety. Comfortable surroundings, including soft lighting and convenient storage, help to keep the caregiver available to the children and in a positive mood.

The physical environment of the child care setting affects caregiver/parent and parent/child relationships. A comfortable place for adults within the children's environment invites family members to visit throughout the day and can also be used to encourage continued breast feeding with infants. A place for adults to sit comfortably for a moment at the end of the day acknowledges their needs and encourages conversation.

The environment affects relationships between children. The amount and arrangement of space and the choice and abundance of play materials can either increase the chances that young children will interact positively with each other or increase the likelihood of biting, toy pulling, and aimless wandering.

The environment can encourage or impede flexible, individualized care in a group setting. With easy access to the outdoors, the daily rhythms of infants and toddlers can be accommodated. Infants and toddlers need small amounts of food and drink throughout the day to support their emotional, social, and physical well-being. A child who is thirsty or hungry cannot interact successfully with other children or adults. A small refrigerator and modest equipment for warming food will allow caregivers to feed infants on demand and offer snacks to toddlers frequently. Infants sleep according to their own rhythms and need their own crib away from the noise of their group (with supervision). A toddler with chronic asthma who needs oxygen can get an immediate response from his caregiver when the tank and mask are kept in a cabinet that is easily accessible.

Sometimes simple changes can make a big difference. The most basic principles of infant/toddler environmental design are also the most powerful:
• create barriers to keep active infants from intruding on infants engaged in quiet activities;
• create clear pathways for infants and adults to move about;
• organize materials in areas that invite children to use them appropriately;
• make it convenient for adults to supervise and carry out daily management tasks.

When Virginia was caring for three young infants, her room's open space, soft, large cushions, and hammock were wonderful. Virginia could easily watch and maintain visual contact with her three babies even while preparing bottles. She and her colleague, Kim, worked well together, watching each other's children, giving each other breaks, and sharing management tasks. Now, Virginia and Kim each had four mobile infants in primary care, and everything was chaos. The eight babies crawled over each other, fell over the smallest toy, and there seemed to be no quiet space to get away. Virginia and Kim transformed the space. They used bookshelves to divide spaces; asked parents to make book pockets to hang on the wall in a corner filled with pillows; moved two long, low benches to create an L-shaped border around the puzzles and small games; and covered quiet areas with awnings made of soft pink parachute material. Once these changes were completed, toys stayed in their areas, and individual babies could be quiet with a book or puzzle, protected from the movement of others.

Our environment speaks to us, telling us what choices we might make, how safe to feel, and whether the events of the day and behaviors of others are predictable. Lighting, size, and configuration of space, as well as the equipment and materials offered, tell us how to behave. Open space invites movement. Since it is the job of mobile infants to practice and stretch their physical skills to the point of risk, they will do that with little regard for objects or people who are in their way. The open room that was appropriate for young infants needs to be rearranged. Clear pathways and defined spaces must be created to channel movement. Spaces for concentrated play with manipulatives and quiet spaces for reading must be adequately barricaded, so that the moving infant must stop before entering. The lighting, textures, and objects in these spaces should say "Sit down, relax. You won't be disturbed here." When spaces are well-delineated and invite certain kinds of activities, they offer clear choices, reduce conflict, and encourage cooperation. As mobile infants move into toddlerhood, a new round of planning and spatial rearrangement will be required.

43

Summary

Excellence in health and safety practices, small groups and appropriate staff-child ratios, primary caregiver assignments, continuity of care, responsive caregiving and planning, cultural and linguistic continuity, attention to individual and special needs, and a physical environment appropriate for infants, toddlers, and their adult caregivers are not achieved—or maintained—by accident. Although the highest quality group care for infants and toddlers may appear natural and almost effortless to the casual observer, such quality requires initial and ongoing evaluation and investment.

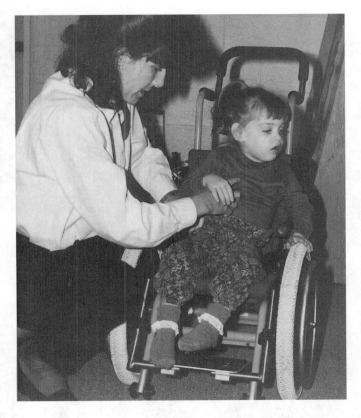

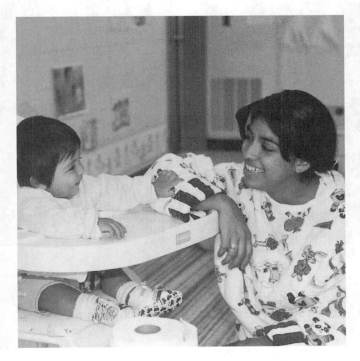

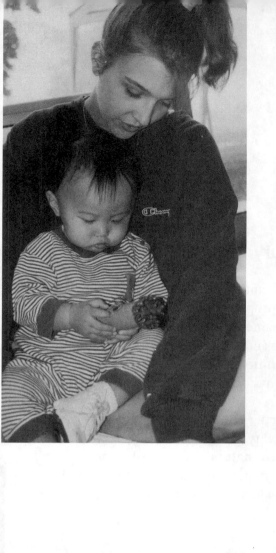

SECTION III

Infant/toddler group care in context:
A constellation of quality

When parents have choices about selection and utilization of supplementary care for their infants and toddlers and have access to stable child care arrangements featuring skilled, sensitive and motivated caregivers, there is every reason to believe that both children and families can thrive. Such choices do not exist for many families in America today, and inadequate care poses risks to the current well-being and future development of infants, toddlers, and their families.

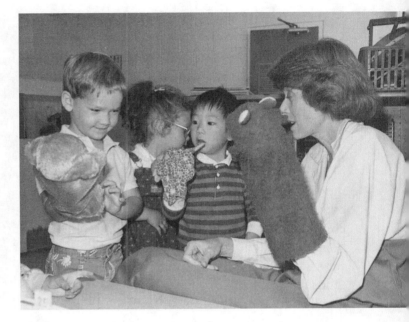

THIS WAS THE STATEMENT ISSUED by a group of leading infant/toddler child care researchers and child development experts convened by ZERO TO THREE/National Center for Clinical Infant Programs at a "summit meeting" in the fall of 1987. Years later, both sentences of the consensus statement remain valid. Skilled, sensitive, and motivated caregivers, supported by strong child care programs and wise public policies, can help very young children and families thrive. But inadequate group care, particularly for infants and toddlers, continues to pose risks to the current well-being and future development of children, families, and the nation.

We have learned that high-quality group care for infants and toddlers can enrich children's early experience and provide support to families. But infant/toddler child care does not stand alone. High-quality care is most effective when it is part of a constellation of comprehensive and individualized supports and services in the community. These services, in turn, enhance the quality of the child care setting. In this section, the quality of group care for infants and toddlers is seen in the context of such a constellation, whose four key "stars" are supports for:

1. child development;

2. family development;

3. staff development; and

4. community building.

1. Child development

Sections I and II of this document have described the rapid pace of children's development in the first three years of life and ways in which healthy development can be encouraged by strong family/ caregiver alliances and components of quality within the child care setting. A comprehensive approach to fostering very young children's development requires, in addition, attention to the child's experience beyond the child care context. Are the child's basic needs for food, clothing, and shelter being met? What resources are available for health supervision and care for acute illness? Who attends to the child's ongoing health, mental health, and developmental concerns?

Because of their enduring and intimate relationships with children and families, child care centers and networks of family child care homes can play an important part in linking families to a range of child development services. Indeed, a high-quality group care program for infants and toddlers should see, as part of its role, supporting families in meeting child development needs that are beyond the scope of the daily child care experience. On-site services, co-location of services, ongoing professional consultation, and systems of referral to high-quality services are all mechanisms through which families, child care providers, and other service providers can collaborate effectively to foster the development of infants and toddlers.

Nutritional needs of infants and toddlers in child care are addressed by the Child and Adult Care Food Program (CACFP), funded by the U.S. Department of Agriculture and administered in local communities. By paying for essential foods, requiring high standards of food handling, preparation and monitoring for compliance, and providing training and information for caregivers and fami-

lies, CACFP assures quality nutrition services in child care settings.

Health consultation specifically designed for the child care context can be a particularly important support to children's development, especially because many families (and caregivers) do not have a consistent source of health supervision and primary health care for their young children. Health consultation models exist in communities and states across the country. Health professionals offering such consultation understand that group care of infants and toddlers poses a particular set of challenges and know that training and advising caregivers and family members is an effective health maintenance strategy for families and young children in the community. They may offer training on health and safety to caregivers, newsletters, a lending library, and a telephone health and safety consultation service. The Resource Center on Child Care Health and Safety at the National Center for Education in Maternal and Child Health collects and disseminates information on these models.

Developmental screening can be offered at the child care site or at another location convenient to centers and family home providers. Universal screenings are non-stigmatizing and offer caregivers and parents an opportunity to share their observations and questions. Both families and caregivers benefit from linkage to local and state early intervention programs.

Consultation from an infant/toddler mental health specialist can be an invaluable support to caregivers, child care program administrators, and families. Fortunately, as understanding of early emotional development and infant mental health issues has increased, more mental health specialists are recognizing the need to help child care settings become more supportive of the emotional well-being

of infants and toddlers, families, and caregivers. Mental health consultation is most successful when the consultant is known to the caregivers, family members, and children. As trusting relationships are established, difficult feelings can be expressed and new ways of relating to children supported. A collaborative effort to assist one troubled child may lead to improvement in the overall quality of care for all children in a setting, as caregivers increase their awareness and understanding of young children's experience and appreciate and value the genuine importance of their impact on the children in their care.

When **referral to a child development service** outside the child care setting seems needed, a trusting relationship with the family helps the caregiver in two ways: first, to discuss the concern and second, to offer information and support to the family. Administrators of high-quality infant/toddler programs recognize that families may need help finding appropriate services and support in dealing with employers when they need to take time from work to take their child to those services. They know the high-quality services in their community, keep lists for referral purposes, and develop collaborative agreements for professional consultation.

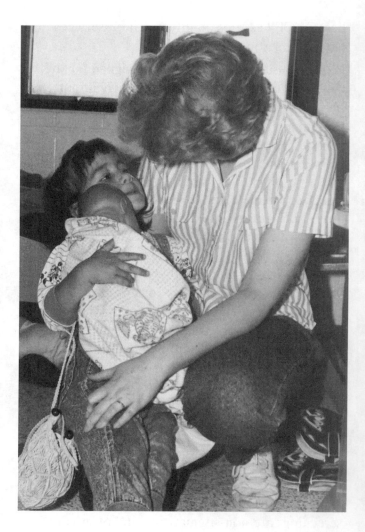

2. Family development

Programs designed to strengthen and support families exist in many different community settings and provide many different services. Several guiding principles unite all those who embrace a family support perspective:

• The basic relationship between program and family is one of equality and respect. The program's first priority is to establish and maintain this relationship as the vehicle through which growth and change can occur.

• Program participants are a vital resource. Programs facilitate parents' ability to serve as resources to each other, participate in program decisions and governance, and advocate for themselves in the broader community.

• Programs are community-based and culturally and socially relevant to the families they serve. Programs are often a bridge between families and other services outside the scope of the program.

• Parent education, information about human development, and skill building for parents are essential elements of every program.

• Seeking support and information is viewed as a sign of family strength, not as indicative of deficits or problems.

High-quality group care for infants and toddlers clearly offers support to families—support, moreover, that comes at a critical time in a family's development. Through program philosophy, policies, planning, and, most important, the day-to-day relationships among child care staff, families, and children, the child care program has an opportunity to put family support principles into practice.

A high-quality child care setting for infants and toddlers communicates recognition of the family as the primary caregiver of the child, respect for family values and culture, and reliance on the families' contributions to the program. Child care center staff or the family home provider makes families feel comfortable about sharing concerns about their child and about issues in their lives that affect their relationship to their child. They offer family members many opportunities to be involved in their child's daily care and education. As a natural place for families to connect with other families, providers of high quality infant/toddler child care encourage the formation of friendships or support networks to help family members with the challenges of parenting and working.

Parent-to-parent support is becoming an increasingly prominent component of child care. For example, the widely replicated Parent Services Program (PSP) was developed to improve parenting skills and to strengthen parents' ability to take charge of their own lives. The PSP model, based in child care centers, gives leadership training to parents and encourages parent control of services. Parents shape the PSP offerings at each site. These may include respite and sick child care, workshops on first aid, General Education Diploma and English as a Second Language classes, ethnic cooking or exercise classes, peer support groups, and workshops on stress reduction, sexuality, or mental health. A parent services coordinator, usually a part-time staff person at each site, is responsible for the implementation of activities and programs. Two especially popular features of the PSP model are family activities, celebrations, and a parent-controlled fund to meet family emergencies. Many family activities and outings, always including meals or refreshments, occur throughout the year. There are also adults-only social events, with child care provided. The parent fund provides small amounts of money to help families in emergency situations. Equally important, the fund provides families with opportunities to share in a decision-making process.

Caregivers who are aware of their important role in supporting families of infants and toddlers make sure to observe how different family members express their feelings about leaving a very young child in their care. They can adapt their style of communication to help each parent feel safe, confident, and in touch when at work. They help all parents understand how important they are to their child. When needed, caregivers can help parents understand their child's temperament and anticipate normal developmental challenges. They know that families differ and take the time to negotiate differences, because they value families as the constant in the child's life.

Administrators of high-quality infant/toddler programs view parents as partners in decision making about program policies and services. The families of infants and toddlers are natural allies with early care and education professionals and child and family advocates in the fight for public investment in quality improvement in child care. Empowered with information, families can encourage and help their own infant/toddler child care providers to meet higher standards of quality. They can also advocate in the broader community for the resources necessary to make high-quality care accessible and affordable for all families with infants and toddlers.

● Staff development

Programs are only as good as the individuals who staff them. High-quality group care for infants and toddlers demands skilled, knowledgeable front-line caregivers and skilled, knowledgeable supervisors and program directors. Research over the past two and one-half decades has consistently linked caregivers' education and training with better quality in early care and education settings. Better quality,

Relationship-focused training programs for infant/toddler caregivers, such as the Program for Infant/Toddler Caregivers developed as a collaborative effort of the California Department of Education, Child Development Division, and Far West Laboratory's Center for Child and Family Studies, emphasize the infant's natural interest, urge to learn, and need for close, responsive relationships with caregivers. Such training stresses that quality care results from a compassionate understanding of a child's development and respect for each child as a unique individual with personal needs and inclinations. Sensitive observation is seen as an essential part of this process. Training is designed to help caregivers and their program managers develop sound infant/toddler group care policies; design safe, interesting and developmentally appropriate environments; give infants uninterrupted time to explore; and interact with infants in ways that emotionally and intellectually support their discovery, learning, and self-esteem.

in turn, has a positive effect on children's cognitive and socio-emotional outcomes.

Core skills for infant/toddler child care staff include observation, communication, management, vigilance regarding health and safety, and planning for the individual child and the group. In center-based care, staff may be at different points in their training and experience, but together, center staff should have the knowledge, skills, and professional competencies necessary to provide developmentally appropriate care for infants and toddlers, and to respect their families' needs, culture, language and child rearing beliefs. Family child care providers can complement their own strengths by drawing on the expertise of colleagues and mentors in professional associations, consultation with community agencies, and taking advantage of formal training opportunities. Regular, collaborative, reflective supervision and mentorship are excellent means for fostering caregivers' ability to observe carefully, formulate questions, and adapt their practice to meet the individual needs of infants, toddlers, and their families.

Families benefit from seeing and being involved in the ongoing process of staff training, professional development, a caregiver's Child Development Associate's credentialing process, or the center's accreditation. They learn to appreciate the seriousness with which caregivers take their professional responsibilities as they learn the complexities of providing a nurturing, safe, healthy environment for very young children.

Most participants in infant/toddler child care training are adults. Adult education principles call for "building a community of learners." This can happen when a trainer works with the same caregivers over a period of time, forming supportive relationships within the group, and providing opportunities in which caregivers become resources to one another. These contacts can then grow into

connections with the broader child care community.

Investing appropriately in the education and on-going support of infant/toddler caregivers and program managers will require comprehensive planning, creative public and private funding strategies, collaboration among training and educational institutions, public support, and an organized, committed infant/toddler caregiver workforce.

4. Community building

The community services available to most families with children under three are few and fragmented. Many families and advocates are calling for organized networks of zero-to-three services. They are also calling for the establishment of a strong, visible institution in each community which could serve as the center of such a network, offering support, information, and referrals to families and to service providers. Such an institution might also offer in a single location a drop-in center for babies and their caregivers (family members or others); playrooms and resources for family child care providers and the children they care for; and a child care center.

Given sufficient resources, the child care setting is well suited to form the center of a neighborhood or community's service network. Infant/toddler child care providers already serve as partners to families with very young children on a regular basis, and over a long period of time. Parent services coordinators and others can strengthen such partnerships, investing the time required to forge links between the program and the larger community of families, service organizations and employers.

When center-based primary caregivers, and administrators and family child care providers build

In high-risk environments, the child care setting can be a "safe haven," potentially the core for rebuilding a community. The Child Witness to Violence Project, based at Boston City Hospital helps young children by supporting the adults who are most important to them—parents, child care providers, and others in the network of helpers who shape young children's lives. Project staff were called by child care center staff concerned about Lawrence, a two-and-one-half-year-old boy who had witnessed the murder of his mother in an attempted burglary in the family's apartment. His father had also been injured as he attempted to intervene on behalf of his wife. Lawrence and his older sister had gone to stay with the extended family for two weeks. Center staff were asking for help in planning for Lawrence's return to the center. The consulting therapist met twice with center staff. The first meeting was devoted to helping caregivers talk about their own loss, sadness, and anger. At the next meeting, the therapist and staff addressed specific questions— what had happened? What behavior or emotional state could be expected of Lawrence? How could staff help Lawrence and his family? How should the issue be addressed with other children at the center? How would the staff manage their own feelings?
Staff needed an opportunity

to face their own horror and grief without having to consider the children's needs. Many were dealing with issues of violence and safety in their own lives. Once they felt it was acceptable—indeed essential—to talk about their own feelings rather than trying to dismiss or disguise them, staff could consider how to talk with the very young children in their care about violence. They were able to use the consultant's practical information to formulate specific strategies geared to the developmental needs of Lawrence and other children at the center. The consultant and staff also planned approaches to talk with parents, individually and in a group meeting. At first, families expressed feelings of hopelessness and of being overwhelmed by the barrage of violence in their community. Family members and caregivers need to express feelings of grief and hopelessness. Often, an outside mental health counselor can facilitate such discussions. Over time, a committee of center staff and families began working with community police, committees from other centers, several faith communities, and elected officials to plan a campaign to transform their violence-ridden neighborhood into a safe haven for children—and adults.

strong, effective working relationships with each other and with other service providers, they are constructing a community that involves and supports the families they serve. Because of their unique relationship to families, caregivers can be a first point of entry into the formal community service system. Because of the unique relationship that develops between caregivers and families, caregivers are in a position to support and, if needed, empower families to access the network of services they need. As child care professionals and families participate together in community planning, they can help to create the network of support that every caregiver and family with young children needs.

● Achieving quality

Realizing the vision of a "constellation" of community supports and services for children, families, and caregivers sometimes seems like a matter of "reaching for the stars." Families and child care professionals have a strong stake in quality. Working together, they may have more power than they realize to bring about positive policy change.

Four approaches to achieving high quality child care for infants, toddlers, and older children can be pursued by child care and other professionals, families, and policymakers in the public and private sectors. These are:

1. investing in the child care workforce;

2. regulation and monitoring;

3. accreditation; and

4. consumer education.

1. Investing in the infant/toddler work force

Competent, well-trained, and appropriately compensated caregivers, supervisors, and program directors remain the key to providing group care that will foster infants' and toddlers' development and strengthen families. The professional development of infant/toddler caregivers can be fostered by:

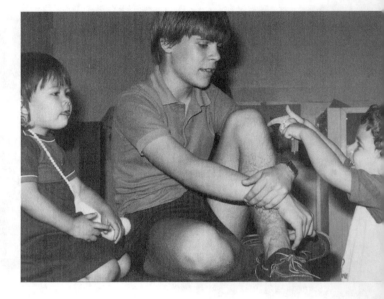

• providing initial training that emphasizes the importance of responsive caregiving and the relationships among infants, caregivers, and families, along with best practice in caregiving routines and health and safety management;

• developing agreements (for transfer of credit, among other matters) among state-recognized educational institutions so that caregivers with varying levels of education and experience can plan a sequence of training and education;

• encouraging certification of the competence of infant and toddler caregivers;

• providing a variety of ongoing training opportunities for beginning and experienced caregivers, aimed both at upgrading providers' skills and keeping them abreast of new knowledge in a rapidly growing field;

• providing supervision and mentorship opportunities, which contribute to the professional development of both less experienced and more experienced caregivers;

• providing sufficient financial subsidy for training and professional development to make them affordable for caregivers and financially viable for supervisors, mentors, and trainers;

• offering specialized training for caregivers (ideally in conjunction with infant/family practitioners from a range of disciplines and settings) in aspects of working with families, identifying and caring for infants and toddlers with special needs, and participation in multidisciplinary, cross-agency teams; and

• ensuring that compensation is linked to training, experience, and level of responsibility.

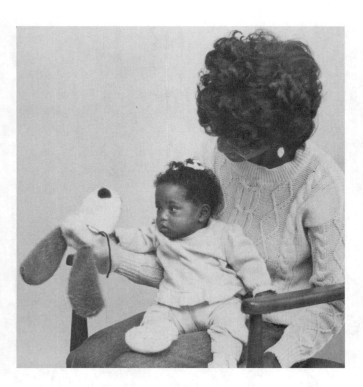

2. Regulation and monitoring

Public licensing, based on regulations passed by the state and/or local licensing agencies, assures some measure of protection for children cared for in groups by someone other than their immediate family members. At a minimum, child care regulations set standards for building and fire safety and for health and safety policies and procedures to protect children, families and caregivers. Research findings suggest that the quality of both family child care and center-based care is higher in states with stronger child care regulations. However, it is no easy task to develop enforceable regulations for child care settings, bearing in mind the developmental needs of infants and toddlers, the demands of parents whose ability to earn a living depends on the availability and affordability of child care, and the concerns of both non-profit and for-profit providers. In addressing regulation and monitoring issues, federal, state, and local policymakers and child and family advocates may work toward:

• setting standards that reflect current research and recognize the serious damage that inadequate child care may cause to the development of young children;

• licensing anyone who provides care for more than two infants or three children under five years of age;

• adopting regulation and monitoring procedures that encourage caregiver self-assessment, train monitors and offer them opportunities to train providers, and encourage consumer education of parents.

3. Accreditation

The National Association for the Education of Young Children's Academy of Early Childhood Programs and the National Association of Family Child Care have created national accreditation systems for both child care centers and family child care homes. These systems require a team program evaluation and improvement process and specify preservice and inservice training for caregivers and administrators. Researchers examining the relationship between quality of children's experience and the accreditation status of their child care program have found that accredited programs offer higher quality and children fare better developmentally than in non-accredited settings. Accredited settings tend to offer staff higher salaries and better benefits and experience less staff turn-over than non-accredited programs.

4. Consumer education

The public, and specifically the families of young children, must have access to information on what to look for in an infant/toddler child care setting. A local or statewide consumer education plan should include the major media outlets as well as local cable access channels, newspapers, and journals. Child care information and referral services now operate in many state and local jurisdictions and perform a variety of functions, ranging from educating parents about available child care options to monitoring complaints about program quality and caregiver practices. Parents who are informed about the child care choices available in their communities are better able to make good choices for their own children or to join with other families, child care professionals, and child and family advocates to fill unmet needs.

Summary

CARING FOR CHILDREN FROM BIRTH to three in groups presents special challenges and special rewards. Through their intense and enduring relationships with children, families, and colleagues, caregivers have an opportunity to make a lasting positive impact on children's lives.

High-quality group care for infants and toddlers is based on knowledge of development in the earliest years—the capacities of infants, the enormous range of individual differences among young children, the origins and impact of different cultural styles of caregiving, and the resiliency with which infants and toddlers cope with developmental change. Because all early development depends in large part on babies' and toddlers' day-to-day experience in their most important relationships, program design, policies, and staffing must appreciate the importance and complexity of all the relationships (child/family; child/caregiver; family/caregiver; among children; among staff) in the group care setting.

High-quality group care for infants and toddlers rests on eight crucial components of the child care setting: promoting health and safety; serving infants in small groups, with high staff-to-child ratios; assigning a primary caregiver to each infant and toddler; encouraging continuity of care; providing responsive caregiving and individualized planning; valuing cultural and linguistic continuity; meeting the needs of the individual child within the group context; and, developing a stimulating physical environment. Excellence in these areas is not achieved—or maintained—by accident. The infant/toddler work force must be appropriately educated, supported, and compensated. Child care professionals, families, advocates, and policymakers must strive for quality assurance through regulation and monitoring, accreditation, consumer education, and, above all, investment in the earliest years.

High-quality group care for infants and toddlers can be most effective when it is part of a constellation of comprehensive and individualized supports and services in the community. The "stars" are child development, family development, staff development, and community building. Infant/toddler caregivers, program administrators, and the families they serve form a nurturing community. By reaching out to create strong relationships beyond the child care setting, the program's intimate community can help to build a larger community of high-quality services and resources to support the healthy development of children and families in the earliest years of life.

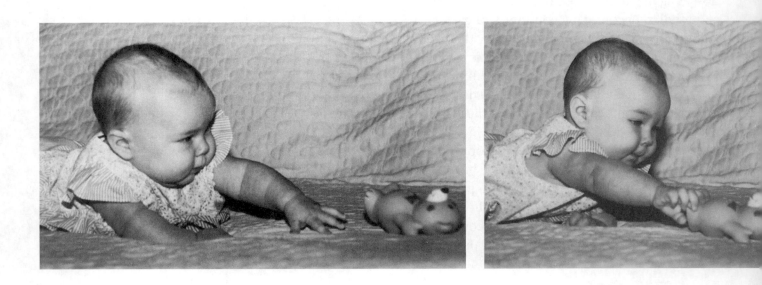

Illustrations of Appropriate and Inappropriate Practice

INTERACTIONS AMONG ADULTS AND CHILDREN

Young infant awakes in his crib, starts to cry.

Appropriate Practice

The baby's primary caregiver calls his name in a soft, soothing voice as she walks over to the crib. She smiles and gives the baby a warm hug, holding and soothing him until he is fully awake. She then tells him "Let's change your diaper," patting his diaper to reinforce the message, and walks to the changing table.

Inappropriate Practice

A caregiver comes, picks the baby up, and takes him to the changing table, passing him to another caregiver, who is assigned to morning diaper changing.

Young infant, lying on her tummy trying to roll over but failing, begins to fuss and then cry.

Appropriate Practice

Her caregiver turns to her, saying in a soothing voice, "Are you tired of being on your tummy?" He gently helps the baby roll onto her back. He looks into her eyes smiling, then makes an exaggerated surprise face and says "Look what you can do!"

Inappropriate Practice

A caregiver tosses a few new toys within the baby's reach. When she continues to cry, the caregiver puts her on her back and puts a teething toy into her hand.

Young infant, on tummy, drools on carpet as she enthustastically gurgles and practices repertoire of sounds.

Appropriate Practice

Her caregiver lies down in front of the baby and copies her sounds. He responds to each sound, then waits, looking into the baby's eyes with anticipation until she makes the next sound. They have a real dialog going. Without missing a beat, he slips a diaper cloth under the baby's head to keep the carpet clean.

Inappropriate Practice

The caregiver does not approach the baby until he sees that she is drooling. He gets a diaper cloth, picks her up, puts the cloth underneath her, lays her down, pats her twice, and walks away.

We use the term "caregiver" for an early care and education specialist working with infants and toddlers in a center or family child care home.

Young infant, being fed his bottle, pats his hand on the bottle and looks at the caregiver's face.

Appropriate Practice

His caregiver smiles, stroking his hand and leg gently. She lets him push the bottle away when he wants a break but she holds the bottle within his reach. When he is ready, he reaches for the bottle and pulls it to his mouth. They resume their peaceful rocking, touching and looking into each other's eyes.

Inappropriate Practice

A caregiver holds the baby without looking at him. He has to turn his head to take a breath. She doesn't respond to his patting. The baby looks up at her, but she is watching other children.

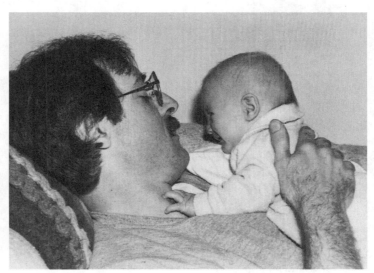

INTERACTIONS AMONG ADULTS AND CHILDREN

● Mobile infant is, fussy because a new tooth is coming in.

Appropriate Practice

His caregiver rocks him in her arms, talking sympathetically to him, touching his lips to show that she knows what hurts. She puts on an audio tape of Haitian songs his parents brought in, knowing that singing and dancing are an important part of his home life. She sings the few words she knows in Patois. The baby seems forget the soreness in his gums as they rock to the music, laughing and singing.

Inappropriate Practice

A caregiver puts on a loud audio tape and tells him to "Sing!" He continues to cry, so she sings louder and claps her hands. When that doesn't work, she picks him up abruptly, shocking him into silence. "You need a nap," she says sharply and puts him in a crib.

● Mobile infant, arriving in her mother's arms, clings and cries when her caregiver approaches.

Appropriate Practice

Her caregiver greets the infant and her mother. "You love Mommy, I know. Today it's going to be hard to say bye bye," and to the mother "How are you doing? Do you feel sad too?" Mother and caregiver talk about separation issues. As they talk, they watch for signs the infant is relaxing, and nod to each other—it's time. There are hugs, more tears, but the baby is ready to let her caregiver embrace her and wave bye bye.

Inappropriate Practice

A caregiver waits for the mother to bring the baby to where she is standing. She takes her from her mother's arms, saying "You better go now. She will be O.K. She stops crying the minute you leave."

● Mobile infant struggles to push a ball up a wide, low ramp.

Appropriate Practice

Her caregiver observes the baby's efforts, smiling at her when she turns to look for him. He uses a few words of encouragement and smiles. She tries for a long time but when she succeeds, she shrieks with pride and excitement.

Inappropriate Practice

A caregiver comes over, takes the ball out of the baby's hands, walks to the top of the ramp and lets it roll down, saying: "Do it this way."

● Mobile infant, watching a friend push a piece of a 4-piece puzzle over the surface of the board, grabs at the puzzle.

Appropriate Practice

His caregiver sits beside them, gently removing his hands from the puzzle while reaching for a similar puzzle from the shelf in front of them, saying "Here's a puzzle for you." He stays to watch them, smiling at the baby as he picks up a piece of the puzzle.

Inappropriate Practice

A caregiver picks the baby up, saying, "No, that's not your puzzle!" puts him down in front of a box of manipulative toys and leaves. The baby crawls back to the puzzle.

FAMILY / CAREGIVER INTERACTIONS

Toddler, joining a group playing with large blocks, pushes a child down who is in her way.

Appropriate Behavior

Her caregiver quickly picks up the fallen child to soothe her, and tells the toddler in a firm voice "Take my hand. No pushing," then adds in a gentle voice "I'll help you find some blocks so you can play with your friends."

Inappropriate Practice

A caregiver grabs the toddler from the back and sits her firmly on a small chair, saying "Time out!" and telling the crying toddler "Get up, you're not hurt."

Toddler, sitting with four friends, asks in Spanish for more apples at morning snack.

Appropriate Practice

His caregiver, sitting with the small group of toddlers, repeats his words in Spanish and says in English to the toddler nearest the bowl "Alma, could you pass the bowl to Juan, please? Thank you."

Inappropriate Practice

A caregiver, standing at the counter, tells him "Talk in English and say please or you won't get more."

Mother starting new job brings her 3-month-old baby to a child care center for the first time.

Appropriate Practice

The family has visited the center and knows the director and the baby's primary caregiver. She knows the center's polices and procedures (e.g., where to put the diaper bag, the labeled bottles of expressed milk, medicine). She has brought a bumper pad from home for her infant's crib, a special rattle, and some family pictures. Her primary caregiver greets her, and they talk as they walk through the morning routine of putting things away and writing on the daily record. The caregiver observes that leaving your baby is hard for most parents and encourages the mother to call, visit and share concerns openly. She lets her know that her involvement will help ensure the best care for her baby.

Inappropriate Practice

Mother and baby arrive and face a room full of busy caregivers and infants. With 7 babies already there, no one notices the new arrivals for a few minutes. A caregiver walks over, holding her arms out to the baby, taking her from her mother. She showers her with kisses, talking baby talk. She tells the mother to put down the bag, that she will take care of everything, and says: "It's easier if you leave quickly so your baby does not see you go."

Morning separations

Mexican-American grandmother occasionally brings her 8-month-old granddaughter to child care, has a hard time leaving.

Appropriate Practice

A Mexican-American woman is the baby's primary caregiver, and she has spent time getting to know the grandmother. She has learned that the grandmother doesn't approve of child care for babies and feels guilty that she can't stay home instead of working. Although the caregiver is often busy she asks her colleague to cover her for 10 minutes so she can focus on the grandmother when she brings her granddaughter. She listens, appreciating how much the grandmother loves her baby and how important she is to the family.

Inappropriate Practice

It annoys the caregiver that the grandmother won't leave. They have asked the director to come out and tell her the Parent Rules about leaving so they are not in the way and the caregivers can do their job. The grandmother does not speak English, doesn't understand, and must be physically escorted to the door.

FAMILY / CAREGIVER INTERACTIONS

● **Father and mother work opposite shifts. The mother brings her 12-month-old to the center very early in the morning, in pajamas and still sleeping. She is rushing to get to work.**

Appropriate Practice

Mother knows that center policies ask parents to have their infants in a clean diaper, fed and dressed for the day. Her caregiver sees that she is really stressed, and tells her not to worry about the policy today. She adds: "I know you want your baby to feel safe and loved by you before you go; but sometimes you just can't do it. Why don't you give her a big hug and a kiss?"

Inappropriate Practice

There is no policy about morning separations. The mother rushes in, puts her baby in a crib and leaves looking sad and frustrated. This is annoying to the provider, but she doesn't say anything.

Evening reunions

● **Father tries to gather up his mobile infant, who clings to the caregiver.**

Appropriate Practice

His baby's primary caregiver knows this father is in a hurry and tired at the end of his busy work day. She talks to him in a gentle voice, saying "Your little girl is still feeling that cold she had, so she's a little clingy. I was just reading my babies this story. Could you read it to her a minute while I bring her things? This is a fussy time for all of us, I guess. I know it is for most infants." The father relaxes as he holds his baby and reads.

Inappropriate Practice

The father rushes around the center collecting his baby's things. The caregiver hands him the baby, saying "She's been awful all day. She wouldn't let me put her down for a minute and wouldn't let anyone else hold her." Father leaves with his crying infant, his voice showing his frustration.

● **Mother comes to pick up her 18-month-old, who has bitten another child again.**

Appropriate Practice

The primary caregiver has called the mother to ask if she can spend some time this evening to talk about how to help her son stop biting. The caregiver's gentle voice reassures the mother that biting is normal for an 18-month-old who can't express his strong feelings in words. They try to identify situations that trigger biting and discuss ways to intervene before it happens and language to use with him.

Inappropriate Practice

When the mother comes to the door, the caregiver greets her with a frown, informing her that "she will have to do something about her son because the children in my program do not bite. It is not allowed!"

FAMILY / CAREGIVER INTERACTIONS

● Single mother in a JOBS program, living in transitional housing, brings in her toddler inappropriately dressed for the snow.

Appropriate Practice

The primary caregiver greets her at the door and asks how the job training is going. Because she knows the mother, she can talk freely. She is careful in how she approaches the issue of appropriate clothing. She notices and remarks that the mother must have put every shirt he owns on him today to protect him from the cold and snow. Very gently, she adds: "I hope you will accept some of the clothes we keep here for the children. Pick anything you like and give it to your son, I can label it for him later. He will be getting the clothes from you, and that will make them special for him."

Inappropriate Practice

In a room full of 16 toddlers one of the two caregivers says to the mother: "You know we won't take him outside like that and that means the other children have to stay in, because we don't have enough staff for someone to stay in just with him. Please bring him in appropriately dressed."

● A 28-month-old boy is crying as he arrives because his mother is angry and embarrassed that he has wet himself.

Appropriate Practice

The boy's primary caregiver gets a little notebook where she has been recording his efforts to use the toilet. She has learned that this family feels strongly about self control and appropriate behavior "in school." Other parents are there, so she gently guides the mother to a sofa, saying softly: "I want to show you something." She opens the book, showing mother and toddler the notes she has on his successes. She asks if the mother can stay to watch him take off his wet pants "all by himself." As he does this, she listens to the mother's concerns, knowing that talking will relax her and give her struggling toddler enough time to show her how well he can take off his own pants. Then they can praise him together.

Inappropriate Practice

The mother takes the toddler by the arm, talking fast as they head for the bathroom. A caregiver steps in front of her telling her in a loud voice that "we don't get angry at our children here." She takes the boy from the mother and carries him to the bathroom, leaving the mother in the middle of the room.

● Out on the playground, the father arrives to see his 30-month-old climbing the ladder to the slide.

Appropriate Practic

The toddler's primary caregiver is watching him as she pushes two toddlers in their T-strap swing seats. She calls to the father, saying that he has arrived just in time to watch a major achievement—the first time up the ladder all by himself. The toddler has fallen before but is determined, and because there is ample shock-absorbent ground cover, she can reassure the father that no one needs to hold him. Father and caregiver encourage him with their eyes and applaud his arrival safely at the top. Down he goes into his father's arms.

Inappropriate Practice

A caregiver yells to the father to come get his son. She tells him that his son is too obstinate, that he always wants to climb on things that are dangerous, and that he doesn't listen. The father picks his son off the ladder telling him in an angry voice to listen to his teacher. She tells him, "Thank you for teaching him to be more obedient."

ENVIRONMENT BY AREA

Diaper area for young and mobile infants

Appropriate Practice

Infants have their own diapering supplies and extra clothes within easy reach of the diaper table. Also within easy reach of the caregiver are: protective gloves, changing table paper on a roll secured to the table, disinfectant stored out of the reach of infants but within easy reach of the caregiver, a foot-operated diaper pail, bags that seal for soiled clothes or cloth diapers, and a handwashing sink and disinfectant soap and cream.

Inappropriate Practice

The diaper changing area is not well designed or organized. Diapering takes time and can be irritating to the caregiver. In the rush to get diapers changed, it is too easy to forget and skip essential steps in the diapering process, like careful handwashing and proper use of gloves.

Appropriate Practice

Diaper supplies and extra clothes are stored in individual, labeled bins every morning. Specific instructions for each baby are noted on a card attached to the bin. As a health precaution, diaper supplies are not shared. The diaper area has pictures of family members or a few other attractive decorations on the wall at the baby's eye level.

Inappropriate Practice

Families and caregiver leave infant diaper bags and supplies wherever they can in the diaper area. Before diapering an infant, the caregiver must find, sort, and get what he needs.

• • • • • • • • • • •

Appropriate Practice

Storage for disinfectants, gloves and plastic bags are clearly labeled. Large graphic reminders of the steps in putting on/taking off protective gloves, proper diapering and handwashing are prominently displayed at the adult eye level.

Inappropriate Practice

Supplies, even disinfectants, do not have a designated space, out of the reach of mobile infants, so adults tend to leave them on the diapering counter. There are no visual reminders of proper hygiene.

Sleeping area for young and mobile infants

Appropriate Practice

The infant sleeping area is separate from active play and eating areas. Babies have their own cribs or cots and their own sheets. Family members bring things from home to personalize their baby's crib.

Inappropriate Practice

Cribs line the walls of the play area. Cribs are all alike and a baby is put in whatever crib is available. Infants do not have their own supplies and there is nothing personal to help the baby feel "this is my place."

• • • • • • • • • • •

Appropriate Practice

Infants who enjoy quiet play as they drift off to sleep or when they awake have a mobile attached to their crib that does not make noise and is designed so the baby can see what is hanging. Caregivers watch for infants to signal when they want to be picked up.

Inappropriate Practice

The caregivers put infants down for sleep or pick them at their convenience. Infants cry themselves to sleep and may cry for long periods before an adult comes to get them.

ENVIRONMENT BY AREA

Feeding area for young and mobile infants

Appropriate Practice

The lighting is dim, but not so dark that the caregiver cannot see every infant. It is quiet. There is a rocking chair (preferably a glider for safety) in the sleeping area and soft music.

Inappropriate Practice

Sleeping babies are easily awakened by bright lights and the sounds of playing babies or loud music. The rocker and cribs tempt mobile infants to use them to pull themselves up to a standing position.

Appropriate Practice

Young infants are held for feeding. If capable, mobile infants sit in small chairs with arms for support. High chairs are cleaned, folded, and put away when not in use. There is comfortable seating for caregivers in the eating area so they can sit with babies while they eat.

Inappropriate Practice

Young infants are strapped into infant seats with their bottles propped on a pillow; older infants crawl or toddle around the play area with their bottles. The high chairs are not folded and put safely away, so they take up a good deal of floor space. There is no place for adults to sit with mobile infants.

Appropriate Practice

Adults label each infant's food, bottles, and medicines and store them in individual bins in the refrigerator. Individual, labeled bibs hang on hooks near the eating area. Dishes and utensils are not shared and are washed after each use. Bottles are individually labeled and washed when finished or, if not finished, are put back in the refrigerator.

Inappropriate Practice

Adults pile infant foods in the refrigerator, and allow infants to share plates, bottles, utensils and bibs. Caregivers spend more time than necessary identifying foods and eating instructions for each infant. Bottles are left out on counters and are not labeled.

ENVIRONMENT BY AREA

Appropriate Practice

Each infant has a labeled daily record book or clip board on a hook in the food preparation area. Caregivers and family members can see it and easily record vital information (bowel movements, feedings, medicines, arrival/departure times, and notes about the infant's activities and moods).

Inappropriate Practice

Caregivers and families have no formal mechanism for sharing information. Adults leave notes on the refrigerator or in the infant's diaper bag. Caregivers may fail to communicate vital information to families.

Play areas for young and mobile infants

Appropriate Practice

Walls are painted in semi-gloss, easy-to-clean paint in a soft color (like ivory or egg-shell). Carpeting and flooring are easy to clean, soft, and of a neutral color. Infants enjoy brighter colors on quilts, thick vinyl mats, and cushions. These add an active feeling to areas designated for active play. Caregivers collect pictures from families and pictures of infants from many different racial and cultural backgrounds, cover them in contact paper, and hang them on walls at the infant's eye level.

Inappropriate Practice

Walls are painted in bright colors and are cluttered with both adult and infant posters. Carpeting is a thick pile, does not provide full coverage of the play and sleep areas, or does not exist.

Appropriate Practice

The play areas are comfortable with pillows, foam-rubber mats, and soft carpeting where babies can lie on their stomachs or backs, and be held and read to. A hammock can be stretched across one corner for caregivers or parents and infants to relax in together. There are distinct areas of interest. For example, low barriers protect infants who are sitting with books or manipulative toys. These areas offer a quiet atmosphere that invites quiet activity. Toys and materials are organized to be visually stimulating and offer clear choices.

Inappropriate Practice

The play area is sterile, designed for easy cleaning, but without the different textures, levels, colors that infants need to stimulate their senses. Or, the area is cluttered with toys and materials of all kinds, offering no clear choices and no protected spaces.

ENVIRONMENT BY AREA

Appropriate Practice

Open shelves within infants' reach contain toys of similar type, spaced so that infants can make choices. Caregivers place activities that go together on different shelves (e.g., fill-and-empty activities are on a separate shelf from 3-piece puzzles, shape sorters, rattles, balls and other moving/pushing toys). Areas for noisy, active play are separate from those where materials require quiet for concentration. Teething toys are indivdually labeled, and caregivers watch to prevent sharing. All toys that infants put in their mouths are washed daily in a light Clorox solution ($1/4$ cup to a gallon of water).

Inappropriate Practice

Much of the floor space is taken by cribs, rockers, and high chairs. Caregivers dump infant toys into boxes, toss them onto shelves, or leave them scattered around the play area. Infants often put each others' teething rings or toys in their mouths.

Appropriate Practice

There is ample, accessible storage for extra play materials of a similar type to what is already displayed and for materials that are more challenging. Caregivers can easily rearrange their space as young infants become mobile. When an infant has explored a toy with his mouth and moved on to other things, the toy can be picked up for washing and replaced with a similar toy. Everything is nearby so caregivers do not have to leave the space to replace a toy.

Inappropriate Practice

Storage closets are far from the infant space and poorly organized, making it difficult to rotate materials, bring out more complex materials, or add to the variety of activities in the space.

● ● ● ● ● ● ● ● ● ● ● ●

Appropriate Practice

Room temperature can be controlled, vents are clean and provide an even flow of air. Floors are not drafty. Windows provide natural light and fresh air. Caregivers carry infants to the windows to see outside.

Inappropriate Practice

Rooms are too hot or too cold, the floor is drafty, little natural light enters the room, and it is difficult to carry infants to look out of the windows because they are either too high or far away.

Appropriate Practice

An outside play area, adjacent to the infant area, includes sunny and shaded areas. It is enclosed by protective fencing. The ground around climbing structures and in some of the open space is covered with shock-absorbent tile to make it easy for mobile infants to push wagons and ride scooters. There are soft areas where young infants can lie on quilts.

Inappropriate Practice

Infants rarely go out because there is no adjacent play area and nearby parks and playgrounds offer no shaded areas or soft surfaces for babies to lie or crawl about freely. Or, inappropriate group size and staff-child ratios make outdoor play difficult.

ENVIRONMENT BY AREA

Interest areas for toddlers

Appropriate Practice

Walls are painted in semi-gloss, easy-to-clean paint in a soft color (like an ivory or egg-shell) Carpeting and flooring materials are selected to provide a soft background so that toddler's eyes are drawn to the materials and activity choices. Wall displays for adults are at adult eye level and are carefully selected. Toddlers' art work and other creative projects are hung at a level just above toddlers' reach but low enough for both children and adults to admire them.

Inappropriate Practice

Walls are painted in bright colors or are sterile and bland. Floor coverings are bright or have patterns that are visually distracting. Walls cluttered with adult and children's posters, and/or displays designed for elementary school classrooms. Toddlers art is not displayed, or is too high for the toddlers to see.

Appropriate Practice

Floor coverings are appropriate for the activities that occur there—shock-absorbent tiles for open areas where toddlers run, push and pull toys around and for art, eating, and water/sand play areas, etc. Low-pile, easy-to-clean, carpeting or non-slip area rugs cover areas for quiet play—book corner, small block play, puzzles and manipulative games, etc.

Inappropriate Practice

Carpeting is a thick pile, does not provide full coverage of the play and sleep areas, or does not exist. Or floor coverings are dirty, or hard and cold. Area rugs/carpeting under water/sand, art, or eating areas requires constant cleaning—or is left dirty.

Appropriate Practice

Caregivers organize their space into interest or activity areas, including areas for active play, concentrated small group play, being alone, arts/water/sand and other messy activities, dramatic play, construction, eating, toileting, dressing, and storage of individual possessions. Shelves and cubbies are labeled and each thing in the room has a place. The areas are boundries by low partitions, shelves or sitting benches, making it difficult for running toddlers to disturb toddlers engaged in concentrated play, and creating clear traffic patterns.

Inappropriate Practice

Space is open with no clear traffic pattern from one interest area to another. Toddlers wander aimlessly, unable to make choices. Fighting and tantrums occur as running toddlers bump into those who are engaged in concentrated play.

ENVIRONMENT BY AREA

Appropriate Practice

Caregivers label each activity area with the name of the activity and a symbol to encourage toddlers to feel in control of their environment and increase their interest in spoken and written words. With low barriers around each area, toddlers know where things belong and can more easily master the task of cleaning up themselves. Pictures of specific materials or toys or shapes glued to the shelves make cleaning up a matching activity.

Inappropriate Practice

Caregivers mix activities that require different skills and behaviors (e.g., quiet activities combined with active toys). Toddlers take materials from one place to another. Clean-up is an unpleasant experience for all.

Appropriate Practice

A child-sized sink with a good supply of paper towels is located near areas designated for messy activities so that toddlers learn that cleaning up and washing their hands follow any messy activity. Smocks are on low hooks so that toddlers can get them themselves. Individual work areas are defined by trays or placemats. Cups, paint cans and other containers are small so toddlers can easily manage them and clean-up is easy. Toddlers can do most activities without adult assistance.

Inappropriate Practice

Caregivers restrict messy activities and do not allow toddlers to explore the texture and feel of the paints or sand. Toddlers must start and end at the same time so adults can put on their smocks and then take them to the bathroom in groups. Messy activities require constant adult supervision and assistance.

Appropriate Practice

Outdoor play is a frequent, daily activity. Toddlers can go out in small groups with their primary caregiver or with the larger group. There is a hard-surface area where toddlers can ride tricycles. Caregivers bring sand and water or art materials outside. Walks around the neighborhood or to a park, treasure hunts, and special trips are planned so that toddlers see many outdoor environments.

Inappropriate Practice

Toddlers rarely go outside because it takes so much time to get organized. Or, they must walk a long way to the play area. Inappropriate group size and staff-child ratios make such expeditions dangerous. Caregivers consider toddlers too young to appreciate field trips.

ENVIRONMENT BY AREA

Daily routines and plans for toddlers

Appropriate Practice

There is a planned schedule of basic routines (eating, sleeping inside/outside times) from which toddlers learn quickly to predict what will happen next. While schedules are predictable, caregivers can be flexible in order to respond to toddlers' interests, moods and needs.

Inappropriate Practice

There is no regular schedule so toddlers can not predict what will happen next. Or, daily schedules are rigid so caregivers do not follow the interests of the toddlers.

. . . .

Appropriate Practice

Caregivers develop daily plans based on their assessment of their group's interests. Planning may involve rotating materials, introducing special activities, new books, new music, or a community exploration. Adults bring out special materials to further the interests of a particular toddler or small group or friends (e.g., expansion of dramatic play props).

Inappropriate Practice

Caregivers either do not plan daily, or have fixed plans they do not adapt to the needs of the children. Caregivers frequently find toddlers frustrated or uncooperative, or engaging in silliness to resist adult direction or as an alternative to boredom.

Appropriate Practice

Caregivers are alert and prepared to be flexible. They adapt schedules and activities to meet the individual and group needs. They appreciate the way toddlers repeat tasks until they master them. They build upon skills and problem-solving strategies they have developed. They allow toddlers to go at their own pace. They have time to assist a child with special needs because the group of toddlers knows what is expected and is engaged.

Inappropriate Practice

Caregivers lose patience with toddlers' desire for repetition. Toddlers must either do things in groups according to the caregivers' plan or follow adult demands that they spend a certain amount of time at an activity. Caregivers engaged in constant direction have little time for a child with special needs.

Eating area for toddlers

Appropriate Practice

Toddlers eat at small tables with a small group. Each toddler has a place mat that is different from others. Toddlers can "set" the table with their place mats, napkins, cups and utensils. The primary caregiver for the group sits with them and joins in conversation.

Inappropriate Practice

Toddlers eat all together and wait to be served as adults rush back and forth with food, juice, milk, and napkins, wipe faces and clean up spills.

. . . .

Appropriate Practice

Toddlers help their primary caregiver carry plastic bowls to the table. After snacks, they help their caregiver clear and clean the table. The bathroom is within view of the eating area, so when toddlers finish cleaning up they can go off to use the toilet and wash their hands.

Inappropriate Practice

Toddlers fight over little things while they wait for their food. Fighting, silly behavior and spills are frequent. Toddlers must finish eating at the same time so adults can take them to the bathroom in a group.

ENVIRONMENT BY AREA

Sleeping area for toddlers

Appropriate Practice
Each toddler has a cot that is labeled both with her first name and a special symbol or picture that she can recognize as hers. Sheets, pillows and blankets are labeled in the same way with a laundry marker. Getting their blanket, lovey, or special stuffed toy is a part of the nap ritual.

Inappropriate Practice
Cots and sheets are used by all children, with no personal items for their cots. Special items from home are discouraged because "children might lose them," or "they will fight over them."

• • • • • • • • • • • •

Appropriate Practice
Preparing for naps can be difficult for more active toddlers, so a transition time is planned with a predictable sequence. Caregivers read stories. Toddlers pick a special book, get their own stuffed toy or blanket and go to their cots; soft music or a story tape is played for toddlers who are still awake.

Inappropriate Practice
Nap time is chaotic as toddlers wander about while adults put out cots. Nap time starts for all when the adult says "lie down" and turns off the light. Some toddlers sleep; others get into trouble or cry.

Appropriate Practice
The toddler nap area can be in the play area as long as cots are well separated from each other. The adult plans where each toddler's cot will go according to the toddler's ease or difficulty in resting, distractibility, need for quiet, or length of normal nap.

Inappropriate Practice
Caregivers put cots wherever they fit in the room. Some are too close together. No thought is given to planning for the individual toddler's sleeping needs.

• • • • • • • • • • • •

Appropriate Practice
Soft music, a story tape, special books (e.g. a small family photo album) or rocking are part of the nap routine because they help the more active toddler relax and fall asleep.

Inappropriate Practice
Caregivers/providers get angry at toddlers who are more active and have difficulty falling asleep.

Diapering/toileting area for toddlers

Appropriate Practice
A diapering area with a sink and toddler-sized toilets are adjacent to the activity areas and eating area. Older toddlers with good bowel control who know how to wash their hands can use the toilet on their own. Doors are open so that adults can see older toddlers in the bathroom at all times. Vivid pictures on the wall remind toddlers of the proper steps to toileting and hand washing. As an added reminder, adults glue a foot print path to the floor that goes from the toilet to the sink.

Inappropriate Practice
The diapering area and bathrooms are not near the toddler room. Toddlers must line up for the bathroom at times dictated by the caregiver. Even the older toddlers with good bowel control may urinate or defecate in their clothes because they are not allowed to go to the bathroom.

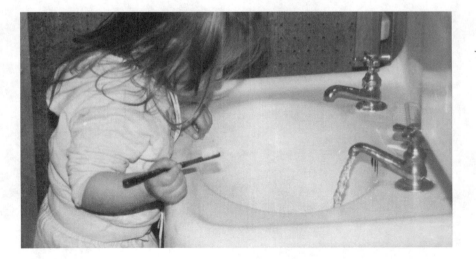

EQUIPMENT AND MATERIALS BY AREA

Quiet areas for young and mobile infants

Appropriate Practice

Each infant has a crib, with bumper pad. Cribs are made of wood, metal or approved plastic. Each has a secure latching device to secure the drop-side. The slats are no more than $2\,^3/_8$ inches apart, and the height from the top of the mattress to top of rail is 36 inches. Cribs are spaced 3 feet apart so infants do not breathe directly on each other. Infants are placed on backs for sleeping. If apnea monitors are necessary, caregiver are trained to check that they are operating.

Inappropriate Practice

Cribs do not meet safety requirements; thus infants are at risk of strangulation or entrapment. Infants can also be smothered by pillows or tight unprotected corners where they can be wedged as they move during sleep.

Appropriate Practice

Thick cardboard books are placed in book pockets or a sturdy book stand. Books that the adults read to the babies are on a shelf out of reach. Books show children and families of many different racial and cultural backgrounds, and adults of all ages. Books made by families or caregivers with cardboard and clear contact paper (or even a box with pictures on cardboard) show pictures of infants' families. There is a hammock, a glider, an overstuffed chair and big cushions where adults can hold infants and read to them.

Inappropriate Practice

There are either no books, or they are tossed about the room with no place for reading. There is no seating where an adult can sit comfortably with infants in her arms and read to them.

Feeding areas for young and mobile infants

Appropriate Practice

High chairs are used only when needed; they can be folded and stored away from the infant area. T-shaped safety straps are securely installed on high chairs. Waist-high tables with infant chairs with side arms are used for feeding infants who can sit.

Inappropriate Practice

High chairs are not carefully selected or maintained. There are no safety straps, and they are not routinely checked to ensure trays will not fall off. High chairs are always out. There are no small tables and chairs to invite mobile infants to show their small and large-muscle motor control.

• • • • • • • • • • • • •

Appropriate Practice

If there is no separate kitchen and kitchen staff, food preparation and eating occur in the infant area. Equipment includes: a refrigerator with a thermometer and bins that are labeled for each infant's food, bottles and medicines; a stove (and microwave); a sink for handwashing; a dishwashing machine and a three-basin sink; ample counter space for several adults to prepare foods at the same time.

Inappropriate Practice

The food preparation area is poorly equipped. It does not allow caregiver to readily identify infants' individual foods and medicines or move about to prepare food without running into high chairs or other adults.

EQUIPMENT AND MATERIALS BY AREA

Active areas for young and mobile infants

Appropriate Practice

Mobile infants have an open area, where scooters, balls, push-pull toys, wagons and other equipment encourage free movement and testing of large muscle skills and coordination. There are ramps wide enough for two mobile infants to crawl up and sit together.

Inappropriate Practice

Scooters and other moving toys are for outdoor use only. Equipment designed for crawling up/down, under/through, is not available.

• • • • • • • • • • • •

Appropriate Practice

Large vinyl mats are stacked for climbing. A crawl-through structure (or just large boxes with cut-out doors and windows) invites hide and seek games as well as privacy. In the carpeted play area, separate shelves are used to display toys for young infants and for mobile infants.

Inappropriate Practice

Mobile infants constantly tumble over young infants, crawl onto shelves or open cabinets, and push around chairs or whatever is available. Young and mobile infant materials are scattered on the floor, thrown together in boxes or tossed onto shelves.

Quiet areas for toddlers

Appropriate Practice

Puzzles, construction materials, and blocks with people, animals, cars, and other accessories are on separate shelves. There are two or more of the same item next to each other. Each set of materials is displayed on low shelves and contained in a bin that has a picture of the item on the front. Small tables, with low shelves near them with similar manipulative toys, invite toddlers to concentrate.

Inappropriate Practice

There are few choices of puzzles, manipulative, and construction materials. Toddlers fight frequently, start building, then move away with some of the building materials in their hands, or wander aimlessly, unable to make choices or unwilling to compete for materials.

• • • • • • • • • • • •

Appropriate Practice

Adults show respect for books and toddlers' need for quiet, privacy, or for sharing a moment with a friend. They organize a display of books in a protected area with cushions.

Inappropriate Practice

Books are either on the shelves with other materials or only available when adults bring them out.

Active areas for toddlers

Appropriate Practice

Water and sand tables are either both available (but separate from each other to discourage shoveling sand into the water), or one table is available and can be used with water or sand. A wide variety of non-toxic art materials made for toddler use is available.

Inappropriate Practice

Water/sand tables and easels with bins that hold paints securely are not available. This kind of play is only done as an adult-directed group activity.

• • • • • • • • • • • •

Appropriate Practice

Climbing ladders, ramps, slides, tricycles, balls, and many other types of equipment are available in an open area both indoors and out. There are duplicates of everything, and enough riding toys for each toddler to reduce conflicts.

Inappropriate Practice

There is no safe space indoors for riding, climbing, and running. There are not enough similar pieces of equipment to allow several toddlers to do the same thing at once. Caregivers must intervene and direct play most of the time.

• • • • • • • • • • • •

Appropriate Practice

The dramatic play area is large enough to allow a number of different types of play to go on at the same time. Parents and caregivers work together to develop prop boxes and change the dramatic play area to reflect experiences toddlers see at home or in the community.

Inappropriate Practice

A traditional house corner provides the only opportunity for dramatic play.

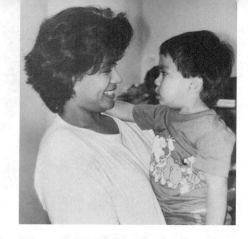

HEALTH AND SAFETY

Health promotion and injury prevention for young and mobile infants

Appropriate Practice

The diapering, sleeping, food preparation, and play areas are separate. There are clearly written sanitation procedures specific to each area. Instructions on the proper diapering sequence (including use of protective gloves), cleaning cribs and play areas, and food storage/food preparation (including dish washing) are displayed on the walls as visual reminders to adults. Family members and all caregivers are provided supervised training if involved in any of these activities.

Inappropriate Practice

Sanitation instructions have not been clearly thought through and are not written down. Consequently, adults forget essential steps in diapering, cleaning cribs and play areas, food handling, and cleaning of food preparation areas.

Appropriate Practice

Each day adults prepare a solution of $1/4$ cup of liquid bleach (e.g., Clorox) to one gallon of water and store it in a place out of the reach of children (e.g., in a closed cabinet) in each area that must be disinfected on a regular basis. All toys that infants put in their mouths are washed in soapy water, disinfected, and air dried before being used by another infant; diaper tables are cleaned after each infant has been changed.

Inappropriate Practice

Disinfectants are left out, not in any special place. They are difficult for adults to find quickly to clean up spills, diaper areas, or bodily fluids.

• • • • • • • • • • • •

Appropriate Practice

All healthy infants are placed on their backs for sleep, even for naps. Research shows that babies who sleep prone, or on their stomachs, are at greater risk of dying of sudden infant death syndrome (SIDS). Because some babies have health conditions that might require them to sleep on their stomach, parents and the infant's health care provider are consulted about sleep position for the babies in their care.

Inappropriate Practice

Child care center has no policy requiring infants be placed on their backs for sleep. Babies are put to sleep on their side, allowing them to roll onto their stomach. Awake and attended-to babies are placed on their backs, denying them the tummy time that is so important for them to develop stronger neck and shoulder muscles.

Appropriate Practice

Health records on infants' well-baby check-ups, immunizations and particular health problems (e.g., allergies) are filed separately for all caregivers and every infant. Caregivers conduct daily health checks for each infant, recording on each baby's daily record form any signs of illness, along with details on eating and elimination. A tickler file is kept to remind each family of upcoming well-baby check-ups and immunizations and to remind adults when they need annual physicals, T.B. or other tests. There are clear policies regarding sick leave for caregivers and alerting parents when infants must be excluded from child care for health reasons.

Inappropriate Practice

Health records are incomplete or outdated. Daily records are not kept or are incomplete. Caregivers and family members are not trained or given information to help them recognize early symptoms of common illnesses and be alert to changes in individual infant behavior that may signal illness or allergies.

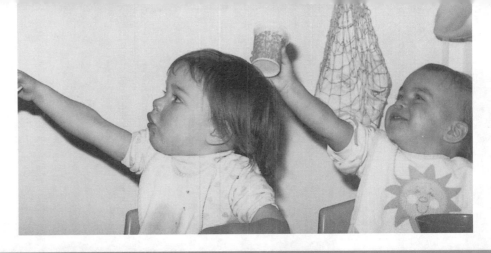

HEALTH AND SAFETY

Health promotion and injury prevention for toddlers

Appropriate Practice
The bathrooms, food preparation, and play areas are separate, and there are clearly written sanitation procedures specific to each area. Caregivers have established and displayed sanitation policies and procedures similar to those for infants.

Inappropriate Practice
Caregivers and toddlers forget to wash their hands before and after toileting or handling food, or they do not do a thorough job and germs are left in the knuckles and fingernails. Germs are spread to the things they touch.

• • • • • • • • • • • •

Appropriate Practice
Adults prepare a solution of $1/4$ cup of liquid bleach (e.g., Clorox) to one gallon of water each day and store it in a place out of the reach of children. All areas are disinfected on a regular basis.

Inappropriate Practice
Bathrooms smell, and there is urine and fecal matter around the toilets and on the sink.

Appropriate Practice
Adults store all foods and medicines properly, in the refrigerator when necessary. Families bring in medicine permission forms signed by a doctor and medication prescribed specifically for the baby. Caregivers record the time, date and amount of medications administered.

Inappropriate Practice
Formal records of medications are not required of parents. Caregivers make mistakes giving medicines or foods to the wrong infant because there is no visual reminder of the needs of each child.

• • • • • • • • • • • •

Appropriate Practice
Families are required to bring in extra clothes that fit the baby and are appropriate for both indoors and outdoors (extra clothes can also be collected and kept at child care). Caregivers dress infants so they are comfortable given the temperature and can move freely.

Inappropriate Practice
Caregivers allow infants to remain in soiled clothing, or in clothing that either is too tight or not appropriate for the temperature.

Appropriate Practice
Adults do safety checks of all areas inside and out several times a day (e.g., electric outlets are covered, there are no objects on the floor an infant could choke on, no splinters or exposed nails on furnishings and equipment, no unprotected pools of water, etc.)

Inappropriate Practice
Adults do not have a system for doing regular safety checks both indoors and outside, so they often do not see that electric plugs are uncovered or disinfectants left where children can reach them. They do not notice paper clips, pins, or pieces of balloon that may have been dropped on the floor.

• • • • • • • • • • • •

Appropriate Practice
Emergency evacuation plans and child emergency forms are on the wall near the infant daily record charts; a bag of emergency supplies is always on hand. Evacuation drills are practiced on a regular basis.

Inappropriate Practice
Caregivers must run around to get what they need for an emergency evacuation. They have no practice in carrying infants, their records, and supplies.

HEALTH AND SAFETY

Appropriate Practice
Health records on well-baby check-ups, immunizations and particular health problems (e.g., allergies) are filed separately for all caregivers and every toddler. Caregivers conduct daily health checks for each toddler, recording on each toddler's daily record form any signs of illness. A tickler file is kept to remind each family of upcoming well-child check-ups and immunizations and to remind adults of their annual physicals, TB or other tests.

Inappropriate Practice
Health records are incomplete or outdated. Daily records are not kept or are incomplete. Caregivers and family members are not trained or given information to help them recognize early symptoms of common illnesses and to be alert to changes in individual toddler behavior that may signal illness or allergies.

Appropriate Practice
Adults store all foods and medicines properly, and in the refrigerator. Families bring in medicine permission forms signed by a doctor and medication prescribed specifically for the toddler. Caregivers record the time, date and amount of medications administered.

Inappropriate Practice
Medicine permission forms are not required. Caregivers make mistakes giving medicines or foods the toddler is allergic to because there is no visual reminder of the needs of each child.

● ● ● ● ● ● ● ● ● ● ● ●
Appropriate Practice
Families are required to bring in extra clothes that fit and are appropriate for both indoors and outdoors (extra clothes can also be collected and kept at child care). Caregivers dress toddlers so they are comfortable given the temperature and can move freely.

Inappropriate Practice
Caregivers allow toddlers to remain in soiled clothing, or clothing that either is too tight or not appropriate for the temperature.

Appropriate Practice
Adults do safety checks of all areas inside and out several times a day to assure that they are safe (e.g., electric outlets are covered, there are no objects on the floor a toddler could choke on, no splinters or exposed nails on furnishings and equipment, no unprotected pools of water).

Inappropriate Practice
Adults do not have a system for doing regular safety checks both indoors and outside, so they often do not see that electric plugs are uncovered or disinfectants have been left out. They do not notice paper clips, pins, or pieces of balloon that may have been dropped on the floor.

● ● ● ● ● ● ● ● ● ● ● ●
Appropriate Practice
Emergency evacuation plans and child emergency forms are on the wall near the toddlers' daily record charts; a bag of emergency supplies is always on hand. Evacuation drills are practiced on a regular basis.

Inappropriate Practice
Caregivers must run around to get what they need for an emergency evacuation, and with no established system or practice, they cannot evacuate toddlers easily and without frightening them.

STAFF QUALIFICATIONS

Basic qualifications for all adults who will work with infants and toddlers

Appropriate Practice

All caregivers express and demonstrate a warm, responsive and gentle way of interacting with infants and toddlers. They talk about children as individuals and demonstrate their respect for individual differences by asking questions about a child before picking him up or engaging in his play. They understand that caring for infants and toddlers requires training.

Inappropriate Practice

Directors hire as caregivers adults who talk about infant and toddler care as custodial work that does not require training.

Appropriate Practice

All caregivers receive orientation training that includes child care policies and procedures and content about relating and communicating with families, health and safety, space arrangement and management. They are observed during the probationary period. Family child care providers seek training and observe other family child care providers, recruiting their help in developing policies and procedures, and their advice about where to get training.

Inappropriate Practice

Caregivers do not receive, and do not seek pre-service or orientation training. They do not consider it necessary in order for them to begin caring for infants and toddlers.

Orientation, in-service and continuing training and education

Appropriate Practice

A training or education plan is developed for each caregiver. The plan is based on qualifications, experience and observed practice (i.e., during the probationary period) and the felt needs and interests of the individual caregiver. The plan includes regular refresher courses in infant and toddler first aid and rescue breathing and on early detection of illness or possible developmental problems.

Caregivers are rewarded by increased status and compensation for major accomplishments in training or education (e.g., successful completion of a series of required training topics, a Child Development Associate credential, an associate or bachelor's degree, etc.). As in child care centers, family child care providers recruit the support of families for caregiver training by talking to them about its importance to the quality of care their child receives.

Inappropriate Practice

Caregivers have no training plan. They complete the minimum of training required by the state or county (if any). Caregivers are not rewarded for training nor is there an effort to educate families about the relationship between training and quality group care.

Developmental Milestones of Children from Birth to Age 3

I Learn Who I Am / I Learn About My Feelings

Birth to 8 Months

I Learn Who I Am

I learn about my body.
I discover that my hands and feet are part of me.
I can move them.

I learn to trust your love.
I feel secure when you hold me in your arms.
I feel good when you smile at me.

I learn to comfort myself.
I may suck my fingers or hands — it soothes me.

I can make things happen.
I can kick a mobile and make it move.
I can smile at you and you will smile back at me.

I Learn About My Feelings

I can show you many feelings — pleasure, anger, fear, sadness, excitement, and joy.
I smile and wiggle to show you I like playing with you.
I frown or cry when you stop paying attention or playing with me.

Sometimes I need you to help me with my feelings.
I need you to try to understand how I feel.
I need you to protect me when I feel overwhelmed or scared.

I share my deepest feelings. I know and trust you.
My smile is brightest for you.
I can protest strongly when I am upset. I know you will be there for me no matter what.

From 8 to 18 Months

I Learn Who I Am

How I feel about myself depends on how you care for me and play with me.
I feel competent when you invite me to help you.
I feel confident in my abilities when you let me try new things.

I am showing you that my sense of self is growing stronger when I am assertive.
I sometimes insist on doing things my way.
When I say, "No!" it often means I am an individual.

I am learning language about me.
I can point to and tell you the names of one or more parts of my body.
I begin to use "me," "I," and "mine."

I Learn About My Feelings

My feelings can be very strong.
I laugh and may shriek with joy when I am happy and we are having fun.
I may sometimes hit, push, or bite because I'm angry or frustrated.

I care deeply about you.
I may smile, hug you, run into your arms, or lean against you to show my affection.
I may try to follow you or cling when you get ready to leave.
I know now when you're gone, and it frightens me.

Knowing when you will return makes me feel better helps me learn about time.
I am slowly learning that when those I love leave, they will return.
A consistent daily schedule helps me know when things will happen.

From 18 Months to 3 Years

I Learn Who I Am

Sometimes, I feel powerful. But independence can be scary.
I count on you to set clear and consistent limits that keep me safe.
When I test limits, I am learning who I am and how I should behave.

I feel good about myself and where I come from when my culture is reflected in my child care setting.
I feel I belong when you speak to me in my home language.
I feel proud when I see pictures of my family and other people like me hanging on the wall.

I sense how you feel about me. Your feelings help shape how I feel about me.
When you respect me, I respect myself.
I tune in carefully to your tone and words when you talk about me.

Sometimes I want to be big. Sometimes I want to be a baby again. And sometimes I want to be both — at the same time. This is one of the reasons my behavior is sometimes hard for you to understand. I don't understand it myself.
Sometimes I will walk. Other times I want a ride in the stroller.
Sometimes I push you away. Other times I want you to hold me close. It's O.K. — I still love you.

I am learning more self-control.
I understand more often what you expect of me.
Sometimes I can stop myself from doing things I shouldn't.
Sometimes I can't.

I Learn About My Feelings

My feelings can be very strong.
I feel proud of things I make and do.
I may be afraid of the dark, monsters, and people in masks or costumes.

I am learning to control my feelings.
I am learning to use words to control my feelings.
I sometimes practice how to express my feelings when I play.

I know you have feelings too.
I learn how to care for others by the way you care for me.
I sense when you are happy and truly there for me. It makes me feel good.

Note: This list is not intended to be exhaustive. Many of the behaviors indicated here will happen earlier or later for individual infants. The chart suggests an approximate time when a behavior might appear, but it should not be rigidly interpreted.

Often, but not always, the behaviors appear in the order in which they emerge. Particularly for younger infants, the behaviors listed in one domain overlap considerably with several other developmental domains. Some behaviors are placed under more than one category to emphasize this interrelationship.

I Learn About People, Objects, and How Things Work	I Learn to Move and Do	I Learn to Communicate and Relate
I can tell the difference between people I know and people I do not know. I recognize my parents' voices. I relax more when I am with you and other people I know.	**At first, my body moves automatically.** I search for something to suck. I turn my head when something blocks my breathing.	**I can tell you things — even as a newborn.** I cry to tell you I need you. I communicate through the expressions on my face and gestures.
I sometimes am afraid of strangers. I sometimes cry if a stranger gets too close to me or looks at me directly in the eyes.	**Within a few months, I begin to learn to use my fingers and hands.** I put my hand and objects in my mouth. I can move an object from one hand to another.	**Within a few months, I develop new ways to communicate.** I learn to make many different sounds. I laugh. I use my sounds, change the expression on my face, and move around to get your attention.
I like to be with you. I like to be held by you. I like you to talk softly and smile at me. I smile and "talk" back to you. You are the most important person in my life.	**Over time, I move my body with a purpose.** I can hold my head up. I can roll over. I can crawl by myself. I may even be able to stand up if I hold on to you.	**I learn to babble.** I make some of the sounds that I hear you use. Sometimes I try to imitate you. I like you to imitate my sounds, too.
I learn about how the world works. I like to look around and see new things. I like to play games with you, like peek-a-boo and hide-n-seek.		**I like to "talk" with you — even though I don't yet speak words.** I may catch your eye and smile to tell you I am ready to communicate with you. I stretch my arms towards you when I want you to pick me up.
I am learning about choice and choices. I have favorite toys and favorite foods. I like to choose what to wear.	**I am learning to do new things with my fingers and hands.** I can make marks on paper with crayons and markers. I can use a spoon and drink from a cup.	**I communicate through my expressions and actions.** I point to let you know what I want. I may hit, kick, or bite when I get too frustrated or angry. I need you to help me learn how to express these feelings in acceptable ways.
I like to see and be with other children my age or a little older. I have fun making silly faces and noises with other children. I do not know yet how to share but I learn through supervised play with others.	**I am learning to move in new ways.** I can sit in a chair. I can pull myself up and stand by holding onto furniture. I learn to walk, first with help and then alone. Sometimes I still like to crawl.	**I communicate using sounds and words.** I create long babble sentences. I may be able to say 2 to 10 or more words clearly.
I want to be like you. I learn how to relate to other people by watching how you act with me, our family, and our friends. I feel proud and confident when you let me help you with your "real work," like scrubbing the carrots.		**I understand more than you may think — much more than the words I can say.** I listen to you and watch you because I understand more than just words. I learn to look at a ball when you say "ball" in my home language.
I learn about how the world works. I am very interested in how the world works. If my music box winds down, I may try to find a way to start it again.		
I am more aware of other children. I am aware when other children are my age and sex. I am aware of skin color and may begin to be aware of physical differences.	**I can do many new things with my fingers and hands.** I scribble with a crayon or marker and may be able to draw shapes, like circles. I can thread beads with large holes. I am learning to use scissors.	**I have many things to tell you.** I may know up to 200 words in my home language and sometimes in a second language. I can tell you about things that happened yesterday and about things that will happen tomorrow.
I like to play together with other children. I may pretend we are going to work or cooking dinner. I build block towers with them.	**I move in new ways.** I kick and throw a ball. I may be able to walk upstairs putting one foot on each step.	**I like you to read and tell me stories.** I especially enjoy stories that are about something I know. Sometimes I may listen for a long time. Other times I may listen for just a little while. Sometimes I like to "read" or tell you a story too.
I am beginning to be aware of other children's rights. I learn I don't always get my way. Sometimes I can control myself when things don't go my way. Sometimes I can't.	**I can handle many everyday routines by myself.** I can dress myself in simple clothes. I can pour milk on my cereal.	**I play with words.** I like songs, fingerplays, and games with nonsense words. Sometimes I can use an object as if it were something else. For example, I might use a block for a phone.
I am becoming aware of how you respond to my actions. I know when you are pleased about what I do. I know when you are upset with me.		
I learn about how the world works. I may be able to put toys in groups, such as putting all of the toys with wheels together. I can find a familiar toy in a bag, even when I can't see it.		

References and Resources

INFANT AND TODDLER DEVELOPMENT

Bornstein, M.H. & Bornstein, H.G. (1995). Caregivers' responsiveness and cognitive development in infants and toddlers: Theory and research. In P. L. Mangione (Ed.). *Infant/toddler caregiving: A guide to cognitive development and learning*. Sacramento, CA: California State Department of Education..

Brazelton, T.B. (1976). *Toddlers and parents: A declaration of independence*. New York, NY: Dell Books.

Brazelton, T.B. (1983). *Infants and mothers: Differences in development*. New York, NY: Delacorte.

Brazelton, T.B. (1983). *Working and caring*. Reading, MA: Addison-Wesley.

Brazelton, T.B. (1992). *Touchpoints: Your child's emotional and behavioral development*. Reading, MA: Addison-Wesley Publishing Co.

Brown, R. (1973). *A first language*. Cambridge, MA: Harvard University Press.

Bruner, J. (1985). *Child's talk: Learning to use language*. New York, NY: Norton.

Chess, S. (1990). Temperaments of infants and toddlers. In J.R. Lally (Ed.). *Infant/toddler caregiving: A guide to social-emotional growth and socialization*. Sacramento, CA: California State Department of Education.

Erikson, E. (1950). *Childhood and society*. New York: Norton.

Featherstone, H. (1980). *A difference in the family: Life with a disabled child*. New York, NY: Basic Books.

Field, T. (1995). Supporting cognitive development through interactions with young infants. In P. L. Mangione (Ed.). *Infant/toddler caregiving: A guide to cognitive development and learning*. Sacramento, CA: California State Department of Education.

Fraiberg, S. (1959). *The magic years*. New York, NY: Scribner's.

Galinsky, E. (1987). *The six stages of parenthood*. Reading, MA: Addison Wesley/Lawrence.

Genishi, C. (1986). Acquiring language and communicative competence. In C. Seefeldt (Ed.). *Early childhood curriculum: A review of current research*. New York: Teachers College Press, Columbia University.

Greenspan, S. I.(1990). Emotional development in infants and toddlers. In J.R. Lally (Ed.). *Infant/toddler caregiving: A guide to social-emotional growth and socialization*. Sacramento, CA: California State Department of Education.

Greenspan, S., & Greenspan, N.T. (1985). *First feelings: Milestones in the emotional development of your baby and child*. New York: Viking Press.

Kopp, C. (1994). *Baby Steps: The "whys" of your child's behavior in the first two years*. New York, NY: W. H. Freeman and Company.

Lally, J. R. (1995). Discovery in infancy: how and what infants learn. In P. L. Mangione (Ed.). *Infant / toddler caregiving: A guide to cognitive development and learning*. Sacramento, CA: California State Department of Education.

Leach, P. (1976). *Babyhood*. New York, NY: Knopf.

Lieberman, A. (1994). *The emotional life of the toddler*. New York, NY: The Free Press.

Mahler, M., Pine, F., & Bergman, A. (1975). *The psychological birth of the human infant*. New York, NY: Basic Books.

McCartney, K. & Robeson, W.W. (1992). Emergence of communication: words, grammar, and first conversations. In J.R. Lally, P. L. Mangione and C. L. Young-Holt (Eds.). *Infant/toddler caregiving: A guide to language development and communication*. Sacramento, CA: California State Department of Education.

Musick, J. (1986). *Infant development: From theory to practice*. Belmont, CA: Wadsworth Publishing Co.

Pikler, E. (1994). Emmi Pikler's first book, Excerpts. *Sensory Awareness Foundation Bulletin, 14*.

Provence, S. (Ed.) (1983). *Infants and parents: Clinical case reports. Clinical Infant Reports Series of the National Center for Clinical Infant Programs*. New York: International Universities Press.

Rosenblith, J. F. (1992). *In the beginning: Development from conception to age two*. (2nd ed.) Newbury Park, CA: Sage Publications.

Sach, J. (1992). Emergence of communication: Earliest signs. In J.R. Lally, P. L. Mangione and C. L. Young-Holt (Eds.). *Infant/toddler caregiving: A guide to language development and communication*. Sacramento, CA: California State Department of Education.

Schaffer, H.R. (1984). *The child's entry into a social world*. Orlando, FL: Academic.

Segal, M. (1974). From birth to one year. Fort Lauderdale, FL: Nova University.

Segal, M., & Adcock, D. (1976). *From one to two years*. Fort Lauderdale: Nova University.

Shatz, M. (1994). *A toddler's life: From personal narrative to professional insight*. New York, NY: Oxford University Press.

Thal, D.J. (1992) Emergence of communication: Give and take between adult and child. In J.R. Lally, P. L. Mangione and C. L. Young-Holt (Eds.). *Infant/toddler caregiving: A guide to language development and communication*. Sacramento, CA: California State Department of Education.

Wachs, T.D. (1995). The physical environment and its role in influencing the development of infants and toddlers. In P. L. Mangione (Ed.). *Infant/toddler caregiving: A guide to cognitive development and learning*. Sacramento, CA: California State Department of Education.

Weissbourd, B., & Musick, J., (Eds., 1981). *Infants: Their social environments*. Washington, DC: National Association for the Education of Young Children.

White, B. (1975). *The first three years of life*. Englewood Cliffs, NJ: Prentice-Hall.

Winnicott, D.W. (1987). *Babies and their mothers*. Reading, MA: Addison-Wesley.

Winnicott, D.W. (1987). *The child, the family and the outside world*. Reading, MA: Addison-Wesley/Lawrence.

Zigler, E. & Finn-Stevenson, M. (1987). *Children: Development and Social Issues*. Lexington, MA: D.C. Heath and Company.

COMPONENTS OF QUALITY INFANT AND TODDLER CHILD CARE

Anderson, P.O. & Fenichel, E.S. (1989). *Serving culturally diverse families of infants and toddlers with disabilities.* Arlington, VA: ZERO TO THREE

Aronson, S. (1989). Child care and the pediatrician. *Pediatrics in Review,* 10 (9).

Aronson, S. (1985-Present, Regular column). Ask Dr. Sue. *Child Care Information Exchange.*

Bailey, D.B. & Wolery, M. (1992). *Teaching infants and preschoolers with disabilities.* (2nd edition). Columbus, OH: Merrill.

Barclay, K., Benelli, C. & Curtis, A. (1995). Literacy begins at birth: What caregivers can learn from parents of children who read early. *Young Children,* 50 (4).

Bemporad, S. & Bergman, R. (1994). Relationship-centered child care: A violence prevention strategy. Dallas, TX: The Child Care Group (White Paper).

Boutte, G., Keepler, D., Tyler, V., & Terry, B. (1992). Effective techniques for involving "difficult" parents. *Young Children,* 47 (3).

Bredekamp, S. & Willer, B. (1992) Of ladders and lattices, cores and cones: Conceptualizing an early childhood professional development system. *Young Children* 47 (3).

Brunson Phillips, C. (1995). Culture: A process that empowers. In J. R. Lally (Ed.). *Infant/toddler caregiving : A guide to culturally sensitive care.* Sacramento, CA: California State Department of Education.

Children's Foundation.. (1988). Better baby care: A training course for family day care providers. Designed to accompany *Better baby care: A book for family day care providers.* Washington, DC: The Children's Foundation.

Commins, D.B. (1967). *Lullabies of the world.* New York: Random House.

Cryer, D. & Harms, T. (1987). *Active learning for ones. Reading,* MA: Addison-Wesley.

Cryer, D. & Harms, T. (1988). Active learning for two. Reading, MA: Addison-Wesley.

De la Brisse, B. (1987). *Children with special needs in family day care homes: A handbook for family day care home providers: Activity and resource book.* (Spanish and English). Washington, DC: El Centro de Rosemount.

Derman-Sparks, L. (1995). Creating an inclusive nonstereotypical environment for infants and toddlers. In P. L. Mangione (Ed.). *Infant / toddler caregiving: A guide to culturally sensitive care.* Sacramento, CA: California State Department of Education..

Derman-Sparks, L. (1995). Developing culturally responsive caregiving practices : Acknowledge, ask and adapt. In P. L. Mangione (Ed.). *Infant/toddler caregiving: A guide to culturally sensitive care.* Sacramento, CA: California State Department of Education.

Dittmann, L. (1984). *The infants we care for.* Washington DC: National Association for the Education of Young Children.

Fein, G., & Rivkin, M. (Eds. 1986). *The young child at play: Reviews of research,* 4. Washington, DC: National Association for the Education of Young Children.

Fredericks, B, Hardman, R., Morgan, G., Rodgers, F. (1985). *A little under the weather: A look at care for mildly ill children.* Boston, MA: Work/Family Directions, Inc.

Garcia, E.E. (1992). Caring for infants in a bilingual child care setting. In J.R. Lally, P. L. Mangione and C. L. Young-Holt (Eds.). *Infant/toddler caregiving: A guide to language development and communication.* Sacramento, CA: California State Department of Education.

Gerber, M. (1982). What is appropriate curriculum for infants and toddlers? In B. Weissbourd & J. Musick (Eds.). *Infants: Their social environments.* Washington DC: National Association for the Education of Young Children.

Godwin, A., & Schrag, L. (Eds.) (1988). San Fernando Valley Child Care Consortium. *Setting up for infant care: Guidelines for centers and family day care homes.* Washington DC: National Association for the Education of Young Children.

Gonzalez-Mena, J. (1995). Cultural sensitivity in routine caregiving tasks. In P. L. Mangione (Ed.). *Infant/toddler caregiving: A guide to culturally sensitive care.* Sacramento, CA: California State Department of Education.

Gonzalez-Mena, J. & Eyer, D.W. (1989). *Infants, toddlers, and caregivers.* Mountain View. CA: Mayfield.

Gonzalez-Mena, J. (1992). Taking a culturally sensitive approach in infant-toddler programs. *Young Children* 47 (2).

Greenberg, P. (1991). *Character development: Encouraging self-esteem and self-discipline in infants, toddlers, and two-year-olds.* Washington DC: National Association for the Education of Young Children.

Greenman, J. (1988). Changing spaces, making places. *Child Care Information Exchange,* 62

Greenman J. (1992). Places for childhoods: How institutional are you? *Child Care Information Exchange,* 87.

Griffin, A. (1993). Caring for mildly ill infants and toddlers in the context of child care: Emotional, medical and practical perspectives. *Zero to Three,* 13 (4).

Griffin, A. (1993). *Preventing preventable harm to babies: promoting health and safety in child care.* Arlington, VA: ZERO TO THREE.

Guilmartin, K. (1992). *Music and your child: A guide for parents and caregivers.* (tape, songbook and guide). Princeton, NJ: Music and Movement Center.

Harmes, T. (1994). Humanizing infant environments. *Children's Environments,* 11, (2), 155-165.

Heideman, S. (1989). *Caring for at-risk infants and toddlers in a family child care setting.* Minneapolis, MN: University of Minnesota Press.

Honig, A.S. & Wittmer, D.S. (1990). Socialization guidance and discipline with infants and toddlers. In J. R. Lally (Ed.). *Infant/toddler caregiving: A guide to social-emotional growth and socialization.* Sacramento, CA: California State Department of Education.

Honig, A.S. (1985). High quality infant/toddler care. Young Children, 41 (1).

Jenkins, E. (1966). *The Ella Jenkins song book for children.* Chicago, IL: Adventures in Rhythm.

Johnston, K., Bemporad, E.M. & Tuters, E. (1990). Attending to the emotional well-being of children, families and caregivers: Contributions of infant mental health specialists to child care. *Zero To Three*, 10(1).

Knitzer, J. (1995, in press). Meeting the mental health needs of young children and families: Service needs, challenges and opportunities. In B. Stroul (Ed.). *Systems of care for children and adolescents with serious emotional disturbances: From theory to reality.* Baltimore, MD: Paul H. Brookes.

Lally, J.R. (1995). The impact of childcare practices and policies on the identity formation of infants and toddlers. *Young Children, 50* (11).

Lally, J. R. (1990). Creating nurturing relationships with infants and toddlers. In J.R. Lally (Ed.). *Infant/toddler caregiving : A guide to social—emotional growth and socialization.* Sacramento, CA: California State Department of Education.

Lally, J. R., Volkert, S., Young-Holt, C., & Szanton, E. (1988). *Visions for infant-toddler care: Guidelines for professional caregiving.* Sacramento, CA: California State Department of Education.

Lane, M. B. & Signer S. (1990). *Infant / toddler caregiving : A guide to creating partnerships with parents.* Sacramento, CA: California State Department of Education.

Lansky, V. (1974). *Feed me! I'm yours.* Deephaven, MN: Meadowbrook.

Leavitt, R. L. & Eheart, B. K. (1985). *Toddler daycare: A guide to responsive caregiving.* Lexington, MA: D. C. Heath and Co.

Lieberman, A.F. (1995). Concerns of immigrant families. In J.R. Lally (Ed.). *Infant / toddler caregiving : A guide to culturally sensitive care.* Sacramento, CA: California State Department of Education.

Mallory, B.L. & New, R.S. (1994). *Diversity and developmentally appropriate practices: Challenges for early childhood education.* New York, NY: Teachers College Press.

Mantutue-Bianchi, M. & Gonzalez-Mena, J. (1995). Culture, communication, and the care of infants and toddlers. In J.R. Lally, P. L. Mangione and C. L. Young-Holt (Eds.). *Infant / toddler caregiving : A guide to language development and communication.* Sacramento, CA: California State Department of Education.

McDonald, D.T. (1979). *Music in our lives: The early years.* Washington DC: National Association for the Education of Young Children.

McLane, J. B. & McNamee, G. D. (1991). The beginnings of literacy. *Zero to Three,* 12(1).

Miller, C.S. (1984). Building self-control: Discipline for young children. *Young Children,* 40 (1).

Miller, K. (1988). *More things to do with toddlers and twos.* Mt. Rainer, MD: Gryphon House.

Money, R. (1995). Enhancing relationships with babies in a group setting. *Educaring,* 16, (1&2).

Moore, S. (1982). Prosocial behavior in the early years: Parent and peer influences. In *Handbook of research in early childhood education.* B. Spodek (Ed.). New York, NY: Free Press.

Mussen, P., & Eisenberg-Bert, N. (1977). *Roots of caring, sharing, and helping: The development of prosocial behavior in children.* San Francisco: Freeman.

Olds, A. (1987). Design setting for infants and toddlers. In C. Weinstein & T. David (Eds.). *Designing settings for infants and toddlers.* New York, NY: Plenum Press.

Palmer, H. (1984). *Babysong.* Freeport, NY: Educational Activities.

Palmer, H. (1984). *Tickly toddler.* Freeport, NY: Educational Activities.

Pawl, J. H., (1990). Self - esteem, security, and social competence: Ten caregiving gifts. In J.R. Lally (Ed.). *Infant / toddler caregiving : A guide to social—emotional growth and socialization.* Sacramento, CA : California State Department of Education.

Pawl, J. (1990). Infants in day care: Reflections on experiences, expectations and relationships. *Zero To Three,* 10 (3).

Pizzo, P. (1992). *Financing family-centered infant child care.* Arlington, VA: ZERO TO THREE

Provence, S., Pawl, J. & Fenichel, E. (Eds.), (1992). *The Child Care Anthology 1984-1992.* Arlington, VA:ZERO TO THREE.

Rogers, D.L., & Ross, D.D. (1986). Encouraging positive social interaction among young children. *Young Children,* 41, (3).

Ross, H.W. (1992). Integrating infants with disabilities? Can "ordinary" caregivers do it?. *Young Children* 47 (3).

Rothenberg, B.A., Hitchcock, S.L., Harrison, M.L., & Graham, M. (1990). *Parentmaking: A practical handbook for teaching parent classes about babies and toddlers.* Menlo Park, CA: Banster Press.

Segal, M. (1988). *In time and with love: Caring for the special needs baby.* New York: Newmarket Press.

Segal, M. (1974). *From birth to one year: The Nova University play and learn program.* Ft. Lauderdale: Nova University.

Stonehouse, A. (Ed.) (1988). *Trusting toddlers: Programming for one-to-three year olds in child care centres.* Fyshwick, ACT: Canberra Publishing & Printing Co.

Surbeck, E. & Kelley, M. (Eds.) (1990). *Personalizing care with infants, toddlers, and families.* Wheaton, MD: Association for Childhood Education International.

The Children's Foundation. (1990). *Helping children love themselves and others: A professional handbook for family day care.* Washington, DC: Author.

Torelli, L. (1989). The developmentally designed group care setting: A supportive environment for infants, toddlers, and caregivers. *Zero To Three,* 10, (2).

Torelli, L. & Durrett, C. (In press). *Landscapes for learning: Designing group care environments for infants, toddlers and two year olds.* Berkeley, CA: Torelli/Durrett Infant & Toddler Child Care Furniture.

Weissman, J. (1983). *Songs to sing with babies.* Mt. Rainier, MD: Gryphon House.

Wittmer, D.S., & Honig, A. (1994). Encouraging positive social development in young children. *Young Children,* 49 (5).

Wittmer, D. (in draft, 1995). The importance of relationships in infant/toddler child care: A unique training program and partnership. Denver, CO: University of Colorado, Author.

INFANT/TODDLER GROUP CARE TRAINING MATERIALS

American Red Cross. (1992). *American Red Cross Child Care Course*. State Chapters.

Bloom, P.J., Sheerer, M. & Britz, J. (1991). *Blueprint for action: Achieving center-based change through staff development*. Lake Forest, IL: New Horizons Learning Consultants & Learning Resources.

Canadian Paediatric Society. (1992). *Well beings: A guide to promote the physical health, safety and emotional well being of children in child care and family day care homes*. Ontario, Canada: Author.

Child Care Careers Institute. (1992). *An annotated bibliography of training resources and materials: Tools for the child care workforce*. Boston, MA: Author.

Child Care Employee Project & Chabot College Early Childhood Development Department. (1990). *Child Care mentor teacher pilot project: Final report*. Berkeley, CA: Child Care Employee Project.

Council for Early Childhood Professional Recognition. (1991). *Child Development Associate Assessment System and Competency Standards: Infant/toddler caregivers in center-based programs*. Washington, DC Author.

Derman-Sparks, L. & The ABC Task Force. (1989). *Anti-bias curriculum: Tools for empowering young children*. Washington DC: National Association for the Education of Young Children.

Dodge, D.T., Dombro, A.L. & Koralek, D.G. (1991). *Caring for Infants and Toddlers. Vol. 1 & 2: A supervised, self-instructional training program*. Washington. DC: Teaching Strategies.

Dodge, D.T. & Colker, L.J. (1991). *The creative curriculum for family child care*. Washington. DC: Teaching Strategies, Inc.

Fenichel, E. (Ed. 1992). *Learning through supervision and mentorship to support the development of infants, toddlers and their families*. Arlington, VA: ZERO TO THREE.

Gerber, M. (Ed. 1979). *Resources for Infant Educarers: A manual for parents and professionals*. Los Angeles, CA: Resources for Infant Educarers.

Gonzalez-Mena, J. (1990) *Infant/toddler caregiving : A guide to routines*. Sacramento, CA: California State Department of Education.

Griffin, A. (1995). *Heart Start: The emotional foundations of school readiness: Trainers' and planners' guide*. Arlington, VA: ZERO TO THREE.

Hall, N.S. & Rhomberg, V. (1995). *The Affective Curriculum: Teaching the anti-bias approach to young children*. Toronto, Canada: Nelson Canada.

Honig, A.S. & Wittmer.D.S. (1988). *The Program for Infant/Toddler Caregivers: Infant/Toddler Caregiving: An annotated guide to media training materials*. Sacramento, CA: Far West Laboratory and California State Department of Education.

Immunization Education and Action Committee. (1995). *Immunizing America's children: A model workshop*. Washington, DC: Author.

Koraleck, D.G. & Colker, L.J. (1995). *Army family child care endorsement training. Trainer's guide to infant and toddler care*. Alexandria, VA: U.S. Department of Army.

Lally J. R., Young-Holt, C., Mangione, P. (1994) Preparing caregivers for quality infant and toddler child care. In J. Johnson & J.B. McCracken,(Eds.) *The early childhood career lattice: Perspectives on professional development*. Washington D.C.: National Association for the Education of Young Children.

Lally, J. R. & Stewart, J. (1990). *Infant / toddler caregiving : A guide to setting up environments*. Sacramento, CA: California State Department of Education.

Rab, V. & Wood, K. (1995). *Child care and the ADA*. Baltimore, MD: Paul H. Brookes Publishing Co.

Segal, M. & Adcock, D. (1993). *Play together grow together: A cooperative curriculum for teachers of young children*. Ft. Lauderdale, FL: NOVA University.

Signer, S. & Stein Wright, S.(Eds.), (1993). *Program for Infant/Toddler Caregivers Trainer's Manual Module I—Social-emotional growth and socialization*. Sacramento, CA: California Department of Education.

Signer, S. & Stein Wright, S. (Eds.) (1993). *Program for Infant/Toddler Caregivers Trainer' Manual Modules I—Group Care*. Sacramento, CA: California Department of Education.

Signer, S. & Stein Wright, S. (Eds.) (1995). *Program for Infant/Toddler Caregivers Trainer' Manual Modules III—Learning and Development*. Sacramento, CA: California Department of Education.

Signer, S. & Stein Wright, S. (Eds.) (1995). *Program for Infant/Toddler Caregivers Trainer' Manual Modules IV—Culture, Family, and Providers*. Sacramento, CA: California Department of Education.

Windflower. (1986). *Second helping training curriculum*. Denver, CO: Colorado Association of Family Child Care.

Wittmer, D. (1994). Advanced Seminars in Child Care Administration: *Caring for infants and toddlers*. Boston, MA: Wheelock College.

VIDEO RESOURCES

Anti-bias curriculum: Tools for empowering young children: Curriculum Guide and Video.(1989). Louise Derman-Sparks & The ABC Task Force. National Association for the Education of Young Children., 1509 16th St., NW, Washington D.C. 20036-1846.

Can I Play Too? (1994) Produced by Partnerships for Inclusion, Frank Porter Graham Center, Suite 300, Nation's Bank Plaza, 137 Franklin Street, Chapel Hill, NC 27514.

Caring for Infants and Toddlers, a video series. Produced by Chip Donahue, University of Wisconsin-Extension. Distributed by AIT, Box A, Bloomington, IN 47402-0120.
- Living, Loving, and Learning: Providing Quality Care for Infants and Toddlers.
- Getting To Know You: Developing Relationships with Infants and Toddlers.
- Follow the Leader: Individualizing Care for Infants and Toddlers.
- Health, Safety, and Nutrition: Building Blocks of Quality Care for Infants and Toddlers.
- Empowering Places and Spaces: Preparing Environments for Infants and Toddlers.

Child Care and the ADA. Produced by Eastern Washington University, Center for Technology in Education and the Community, Paulson Building, Suite 421, West 407 Riverside Road, Spokane, WA 99201.

Let Babies Be Babies: Caring for Infants and Toddlers with Love and Respect, a video series. Project coordinated by Jamie L. Kosbyk. Distributed by The Family Day Care Association of Manitoba, 203-942 St. Mary's Road, Winnipeg, Manitoba, Canada R2M 3R5.
- Rethinking Infants and Toddlers.
- Keeping Babies Healthy and Safe: Part I and II.
- Helping Babies Learn.
- Guiding the Journey to Independence.
- Understanding the Partnership with Parents.
- Caring for the Caregiver.

My Kind of Place: Identifying Quality Infant/Toddler Care. Produced by the Quality Care for Infants and Toddlers Project of Greater Minneapolis Day Care Association. Distributed by Greater Minneapolis Day Care Association, 1628 Elliot Avenue South, Minneapolis, MN 55404.

The Program for Infant/Toddler Caregivers, Video Series, J. Ronald Lally, Executive Producer. California Department of Education, P.O. Box 944271, Sacramento, CA 95812-0271:
- 1995. Protective Urges: Working with the Feelings of Parents and Caregivers.
- 1992. Essential Connections: 10 Keys to Culturally Sensitive Child Care.
- 1991. Discoveries in Infancy: Cognitive Development and Learning.
- 1991. Together in Care: Meeting the Intimacy Needs of Infants and Toddlers in Groups.
- 1989. Flexible, Fearful or Feisty: The Different Temperaments of Infants and Toddlers.
- 1989. It's Not Just Routine: Diapering, Feeding and Napping Infants and Toddlers.
- 1989. The Three Ages of Infancy: Caring for Young, Mobile and Older Infants.
- 1988. Space to Grow: Creating a Child Care Environment for Infants & Toddlers.
- 1988. Getting in Tune: Creating Nurturing Relationships with Infants and Toddlers.
- 1987. Respectfully Yours: Magda Gerber's Approach to Professional Infant/Toddler Care.
- 1986. First Moves: Welcoming a Child to a New Caregiving Setting.

Reducing the Risk.(1994). Produced by Early Childhood Directors Association, 450 N. Syndicate, Suite 5, St. Paul, MN 55104-4125.

Second Helping Training Curriculum and video series. Windflower, Colorado Association of Family Child Care. Denver, CO.

See How They Move. Produced by Resources for Infant Educarers (RIE), 1550 Murray Circle, Los Angeles, CA 90026.

We All Belong: Multicultural Child Care That Works. Produced and distributed by Redleaf Press, 450 North Syndicate, Suite 5, St. Paul, MN 55104-4125.

Yes, You Can Do It (1995). Caring for infants and toddlers with disabilities in a family child care setting. Produced by The Children's Foundation, 733 15th Street, N.W., Suite 505, Washington, D.C. 20005.

MAJOR REPORTS AND RESEARCH ON INFANT/TODDLER CHILD CARE

Adams, G. (1990). *Who knows how safe? The status of state efforts to ensure quality child care.* Washington, DC: Children's Defense Fund.

American Public Health Association & The American Academy of Pediatrics. (1992). *Caring for our children: National standards, guidelines for health and safety in out-of-home-child care.* Updated version available through the National Center for Education in Maternal and Child Health, 2000 15th St. N., Suite 700, Arlington, VA 22210.

Bredekamp, S. (ed., 1987 expanded edition). *Developmentally appropriate practice in early childhood programs serving children from birth through age 8.* Washington, DC: National Association for the Education of Young Children.

Carnegie Task Force on Meeting the Needs of Young Children. (1994). *Starting points: Meeting the needs of our youngest children.* New York, NY: Carnegie Corporation of New York.

Center for Career Development in Early Care and Education. (1994). *Making a career of it: State of the states report.* Boston, MA. Author.

Chang, H.N-L. & Sakai, L. (1993). *Affirming Children's Roots: Cultural and linguistic diversity in early care and education.* San Francisco, CA: California Tomorrow.

Children's Defense Fund (1995). *The state of America's children 1995: Yearbook.* Washington D.C.: Children's Defense Fund.

The Cost, Quality and Child Care Outcomes Study Team. (1995). *Cost, quality, and child care outcomes in child care centers.* Denver, CO: Economics Department, University of Colorado at Denver.

Family Child Care Quality Criteria Project, Frank Porter Graham Child Development Center. (1995). *Quality criteria for family child care.* Washington DC: The National Association for Family Child Care.

Galinsky, E., Howes, C., Kontos, S. & Shinn, M. (1994). *The study of children in family child care and relative care: Highlights and findings.* New York, NY: Families and Work Institute.

Harms, T. & Cryer, D. (1994). *Infant Child Care Environment Rating Scale.* New York, NY: Teachers College Press.

Harms, T. & Cryer, D. (1984). *Family Day Care Rating Scale.* New York, NY: Teachers College Press.

Howes, C. (1991). Research in review: Infant child care. *Young Children,* 44 (6).

Kamerman, S. & Kahn, A. (1994). *A welcome for every child. child care, education and family support for infants and toddlers in Europe.* Arlington, VA: ZERO TO THREE.

Lally, J. R., Mangione, P. L., & Honig, A. (1988). The Syracuse University Family Development Research Program: Long-Range impact of an early intervention with low-income children and their families. In D. Powell (Ed.). *Parent education in early childhood intervention: Emerging directions in theory, research and practice.* Norwood, NJ: Ablex.

Lally, J.R., Mangione, P.L., Honig, A.S. & Wittmer, D.S. (1988). More pride, less delinquency: Findings from ten-year follow-up study of the Syracuse University Family Development Research Program. *Zero To Three,* 13 (4).

Lally, J. R., Honig, A., & Horsburgh, D. (1982). Personal social adjustment of school children after five years in a family enrichment program. *Child Care Research Quarterly,* Vol II.

Lally, J., Provence, S., Szanton, E., Weissbourd, B. (1987). Developmentally appropriate care for children birth to age three. In S. Bredekamp (Ed.). *Developmentally appropriate practice in early childhood programs serving children birth to age 8.* Washington, DC: National Association for the Education of Young Children.

Larner, M. (1994). *In the neighborhood: Programs that strengthen family day care for low-income families.* New York, NY: National Center for Children in Poverty.

Larner, M. (1995). *Linking family support and early childhood programs: Issues, experiences, opportunities.* Chicago, IL: Family Resource Coalition.

Lazar, I., Darlington, R., Murray, H., Royce, J. & Snipper, A. (1982). Lasting effects of early education: A report from the consortium for longitudinal studies. *Monographs of the Society for Research in Child Development,* 47 (2-3, Serial no. 195).

Leach, P. (1994). *Children first.* New York, NY: Knopf.

Modigliani, K. (1990). *Assessing the quality of family child care—A comparison of five instruments.* Boston, MA: The Family Child Care Project.

Modigliani, K. (Ed.) (1993). *Readings in professional development in family child care - project-to-project* Compiled, 1993. Boston, MA: The Family Child Care Project.

Modigliani, K. (1993). *Child care as an occupation in a culture of indifference.* Boston, MA: The Family Child Care Project.

National Academy of Early Childhood Programs. (1984). *Accreditation Criteria and Procedures and The Guide to Accreditation.* Washington DC: National Association for the Education of Young Children.

National Association for the Education of Young Children, (1992). *The supply and demand for child care.* Washington D.C.: National Association for the Education of Young Children.

National Association of Family Child Care. (1985, currently being revised). *Accreditation criteria and self study guide for family day careproviders.* Washington DC: Author.

Osofsky, J. & Fenichel, E.(Eds.) (1994) *Caring for infants and toddlers in violent environments: Hurt, healing, and hope.* Arlington, VA: ZERO TO THREE.

Ruopp, R., J. Travers, F. Glantz, & C. Coelen. (1979). *Children at the center. Final report of the National Day Care Study. Vol. 1.* Cambridge, MA: Abt Associates.

Whitebook, M., Howes, C., Phillips, D. (1989). *The National child care staffing study: Who cares? Child care teachers and the quality of care in America.* Oakland, CA: The Child Care Employee Project.

Whitebook, M., Howes, C., Phillips, D. (1993). *The national child care staffing study revisited: Four years in the life of center-based child care.* Oakland, CA: The Child Care Employee Project.

Willer, B., Hofferth, S., Kisker, E., Divine-Hawkins, P., Farquar, E. & Glantz, F. (1991). *The demand and supply of child care in 1990: Joint findings from the National Child Care Survey and a profile of child care settings.* Washington, DC: National Association for the Education of Young Children.

Willer, B. (Ed.)(1990). *Reaching the full cost of quality in early childhood programs.* Washington, DC: National Association for the Education of Young Children.

ZERO TO THREE (1992). *Heart Start: The emotional foundations of school readiness.* Arlington, VA: Author.

ZERO TO THREE (1988). *Infants, families and child care: Toward a research agenda.* Arlington, VA: Author.

For more resources,
visit www.zerotothree.org

NATIONAL INFORMATION RESOURCES

Better Baby Care Campaign
http://www.betterbabycare.org
The Better Baby Care Campaign, a nationwide effort to improve the quality of infant and toddler child care, provides up-to-date information on research and resources around infant and toddler care. The Web site also provides information on federal, state, and local policy initiatives.

Brazelton Touchpoints Center
http://www.touchpoints.org
Touchpoints Model is a training program for multi-disciplinary professionals. Its goal is to provide them with skills and strategies with which they can build alliances with parents of children aged birth to 3 years. The Touchpoints framework focuses on key points in the development of infants, toddlers, and their families.

Child Care Bureau, Administration for Children and Families, U.S. Department of Health and Human Services
http://www.acf.hhs.gov/programs/ccb/
The Child Care Bureau is dedicated to enhancing the quality, affordability, and availability of child care for all families. The Child Care Bureau administers federal funds to states, territories, and tribes to assist low-income families in accessing quality child care for children when the parents work or participate in education or training.

Child Care Aware
http://childcareaware.org
Child Care Aware is a program of the National Association of Child Care Resource and Referral Agencies and is funded through a cooperative agreement with the Child Care Bureau, Administration for Children and Families, U.S. Department of Health and Human Services. Child Care Aware is committed to helping parents find the best information on locating quality child care and child care resources in their community.

Early Childhood Focus
http://www.earlychildhoodfocus.org
A Web site funded by the National Association of Child Care Resource and Referral Agencies (NACCRRA) to provide up-to-date news items in relation to early childhood education. NACCRRA reviews articles for appropriateness, however they do not guarantee the accuracy of the information. Visitors to the site are encouraged to post articles if they are relevant to early childhood education professionals.

Early Head Start National Resource Center
http://www.ehsnrc.org
The Early Head Start National Resource Center is operated by ZERO TO THREE in collaboration with WestEd. The Center works in partnership with infant–toddler specialists at regionally based quality improvement centers to ensure that EHS programs have information and training on best practices on a range of topics important to the designing and delivering services to pregnant women and to children from birth to 3 years of age and their families. The Web site features a wealth of information for program leaders, direct service providers, and parents.

Healthy Child Care America
http://www.healthychildcare.org
The Healthy Child Care America (HCCA) program is a collaborative effort of health professionals, child care providers, and families working to improve the health and safety of children in child care. Launched in 1995, HCCA seeks to maximize the health, safety, well-being, and developmental potential of all children so that each child experiences quality child care within a nurturing environment and has a medical home.

I Am Your Child
http://www.iamyourchild.org
The I Am Your Child Foundation is a national, non-profit, non-partisan organization that was founded in 1997 to raise awareness about the importance of early childhood development and school readiness. IAYC develops a wide variety of resources for parents, early childhood professionals, child advocates, health care providers, policymakers, and the media. IAYC also promotes public policies that help ensure that children have the physical well-being and the social, emotional, and cognitive abilities they need to enter school ready to succeed.

Maternal and Child Health Bureau, Department of U.S. Health and Human Services
http://www.mchb.hrsa.gov
The Maternal and Child Health Bureau provides links to resources, publications, Web sites, and federal and state programs relating to the health and wellbeing of infants, children, adolescents, pregnant women, and their families. MCHB provides a good list of child health links, including for children with special needs.

National Association for the Education of Young Children (NAEYC)
http://www.naeyc.org
Provides information on accredited child care programs.

National Black Child Development Institute
http://www.nbcdi.org
A nonprofit organization that provides and supports programs, workshops, and resources for African American children, their parents, and communities in such issues as early health and education, child welfare, and parenting.

National Center for Children in Poverty (NCCP)
http://www.nccp.org/it/
The National Center for Children in Poverty's Infant and Toddler Project focuses on the experiences of 25 selected initiatives across the country to provide a menu of concrete, innovative strategies other states and communities can use to promote more targeted and effective policy and practice attention to infants and toddlers. The Web site highlights the 25 communities and shares their creative solutions and five overarching strategies and also identifies resources for policy makers.

National Child Care Information Center (NCCIC)
http://www.nccic.org/cctopics/infants.html
A project of the Child Care Bureau, this national resource links information and people to complement, enhance, and promote the child care delivery system, working to ensure that all children and families have access to high-quality comprehensive services. This link is for publications and organizational resources that pertain to infants and toddlers.

National Information Center for Children and Youth with Disabilities
http://www.nichcy.org
NICHCY is the national information center that provides information on disabilities and disability-related issues pertaining to children and youth (birth to age 22 years). Their Web site provides excellent state resources and contacts.

National Infant & Toddler Child Care Initiative
http://nccic.org/itcc/
The National Infant & Toddler Child Care Initiative is designed to support Child Care Development Fund (CCDF) State and Territory Administrators in their efforts to effect system-wide improvements in infant and toddler child care. The Initiative is funded by the Child Care Bureau, Administration for Children and Families, Department of Health and Human Services and is located at ZERO TO THREE.

The Program for Infant Toddler Caregivers (PITC)
http://www.pitc.org
The goal of PITC is to help caregivers recognize the crucial importance of giving tender, loving care and assisting in the infants' intellectual development through an attentive reading of each child's cues. The PITC's videos, guides, and manuals are designed to help child care managers and caregivers become sensitive to infants' cues, connect with their family and culture, and develop responsive, relationship-based care.

ZERO TO THREE: National Center for Infants, Toddlers and Families
http://www.zerotothree.org
ZERO TO THREE's award-winning Web site offers a multitude of resources and information for parents and for p_____ ___ ___ sources include the full te__ __selected articles from its bimonthly Jou____l; the Brain Wonders section, featuring ___e latest information on early brain development; and other resources on topics from A to Z.